The Patron

Elizabeth Hassan

Copyright ©2025 by Elizabeth Hassan.

All Rights Reserved.

Table of Contents

Dedications i
Acknowledgments ii
About the Author iii
Prologue iv
Chapter 1: The Voice 1
Chapter 2: The Forgotten Prophecy 14
Chapter 3: The Vision 27
Chapter 4: The Stranger 36
Chapter 5: The King 49
Chapter 6: The Suitors 62
Chapter 7: The Drunk 71
Chapter 8: The Trick 84
Chapter 9: The Letter 101
Chapter 10: The Reckoning 121
Chapter 11: The Crown 151
Chapter 12: The Endgame 169

Dedications

To benevolence—

The quiet strength that changes lives without needing recognition.

Acknowledgments

To all the people who have shown me love and care throughout my life—

Your kindness has been my compass, my comfort, and my reason to keep going.

About the Author

Elizabeth Hassan is a South Asian writer with a postgraduate degree in English Literature and a background in business administration. Her professional and personal journey has taken her across many cultures, allowing her to explore diverse histories, philosophies, and worldviews.

With a deep interest in the rise and fall of civilizations, Elizabeth has spent years studying what makes a society truly successful. Her reflections have led her to a simple but powerful conclusion: the most enduring civilizations are those built on justice, fairness, and strong moral character.

Among the many historical figures she has studied, Elizabeth holds a special admiration for the Prophet Muhammad (peace be upon him), whose example of compassion and integrity continues to inspire her. His life has shaped her belief in the importance of respecting the benevolence of people from all backgrounds.

At the heart of her writing and worldview is a core value: gratitude. For Elizabeth, gratitude is more than words—it is a sincere action. It is a way to honour others and nurture peace in a world that often forgets to pause and appreciate the good.

Prologue

There are stories that have been passed down for generations, stories about beings called the jinn. These creatures come from a world that's just out of sight, not quite like anything we know.

They are said to be made of smokeless fire, and while they can be kind, they can also be mischievous or even dangerous. What makes them so mysterious is that they exist in a land close to ours but just far enough away to make you wonder whether they are real at all.

The jinn, according to the old tales, can enter our world in ways we might not even notice. Some are said to be playful, like children hiding your keys or making strange noises in the night.

Others are darker, hiding in the shadows, whispering things into your mind that don't feel like your own thoughts. They're like dreams that feel too real or memories that aren't yours. And sometimes, they make promises. Big promises. Promises of love, riches, or even power. But you have to be careful because the jinn never give anything without asking for something in return.

Throughout history, people have warned against getting too close to the jinn. "Don't speak to them," they say. "Don't listen to their sweet words." And yet, in the quiet moments of life, when your mind wanders or when you're alone, the jinn might find their way to you. They are clever, slipping in when you least expect it, and once they've got your attention, they don't let go easily.

Some people say it's all in your mind. They believe that the jinn are just a part of our imagination, a way for our fears and desires to take shape. Others say the jinn are real, that they walk among us, watching and waiting for the right moment to make their move. Maybe it's somewhere between the two, where what you believe shapes what you see.

This is the story of one person who found herself caught between these worlds. It's a story of how a single whisper, a thought that wasn't quite her own, changed everything. It's about the line between what is real and what isn't, about dreams that blur with waking life.

You see, the jinn don't always announce themselves. They don't make loud, dramatic entrances. Instead, they slip into your thoughts like a soft breeze. But once they've taken hold, it's hard to tell where their words end and your own thoughts begin.

Be careful. This is a story that doesn't give easy answers. It is about what happens when we let our imaginations take the lead, and where that might take us.

So, listen closely. Pay attention to the whispers in the dark. You might just find that they have more to say than you think.

The jinn are waiting.

Chapter 1: The Voice

October 12, 2004

Layla was walking through her house – her house. It was familiar in every way, but somehow different. It was her house, no doubt about that, yet something felt off. The stillness of it was unsettling. Her mom was always home, always filling the space with noise, movement, life. But today, the house was silent. Empty.

The cold was the next thing she noticed. There was a strange chill in the air, colder than it had ever been. Usually, she would shrug it off as a draft, but right now, it felt like it was something deeper. It didn't make much sense to her, but the house somehow felt cold and distant.

As Layla turned the corner, her feet moved almost on their own, pulling her toward the attic. She'd always avoided it. The attic had always made her uneasy, but now, she couldn't shake the feeling that she had to go up there.

The hallway grew darker, colder with every step she took. Suddenly, a gust of wind swept through, slamming all the windows and doors shut with a force that made Layla flinch. Goosebumps prickled on her arms. She reached up, about to touch them, but then—

'Layla.'

The whisper came from nowhere, yet it felt as if it were right next to her. She spun around with a racing, but there was no one there. No movement, no sound. Just silence again.

Then, without warning, the scene changed. The walls, the cold, the house—gone. Layla found herself standing in the middle of nowhere. In the distance, she saw the storm, dark and fast, creeping toward her.

Terrified, she turned and ran, but her legs felt like they were moving through thick mud. She couldn't run fast enough. The storm was getting closer, and her body refused to keep up with the panic in her chest.

'Layla.'

The voice came again, sharp, like a hiss, and this time, it was so close it almost felt like it was in her ear. Terrified, she pushed herself harder, but her feet stumbled over a rock and sent her crashing to the ground.

'You will marry a prince one day,' The voice whispered before everything went black.

"Layla!"
"Layla! Open your eyes!"

Layla's eyes snapped open. Her forehead was damp with sweat, and her heart raced in her chest. The room was dark, with only a sliver of light coming through the curtains. It was still night.

Just a bad dream. That's all it was.

Her mother was sitting beside her with concern evident in her eyes. Layla's breathing was fast, her body was shaking, and her mind was foggy. She could hardly focus.

"Layla, darling, what happened?" her mother asked gently. "You were screaming."

Layla took a deep breath, trying to calm herself. It felt like the nightmare had only just left her, but she couldn't remember it clearly anymore. Only that voice. That strange voice.

"Just a bad dream," Layla said quietly, though she wasn't sure if she believed it herself.

Her mother wasn't entirely convinced either. She looked at Layla with concerned eyes and gently held her hand. "Are you sure? You've been having these dreams a lot lately. I'm starting to get worried."

If truth be told, Layla was worried, too. The first time it happened, she narrated the entire dream to her mother. The look on her face was enough for Layla to realise she should never speak about these nightmares again. She didn't want to worry her mother; the woman already had a lot on her plate.

Layla nodded. She didn't know how to explain it. How could she tell her mother about the feeling? How does she find the words to describe the strange sense that something was wrong? And how could she explain the voice that had whispered in her ear, over and over: *"You will marry a prince."*

It felt so real. Too real.

"I'm fine," Layla muttered. "Really, I'm okay."

"I think we should go see someone, Layla. Maybe a doctor or… someone who can help."

Layla slowly sat up and rubbed her eyes. She wasn't entirely sure what was happening to her. On the outside, they were just nightmares. But deep down, Layla knew something was gradually taking over her.

"I don't think so, Mum," she said. She didn't want to make a big deal of it. She's old enough to handle this on her own. But could she?

Her mind was racing. The room was back to being silent, but Layla could sense a strange heaviness in the air. And that menacing voice… it still echoed in her ears.

"You will marry a prince."

The more she thought about it, the stranger it felt. It was just a silly thought, wasn't it? Yet, somehow, she wasn't able to push it away.

What did it even mean?

With her mind swarming with questions that had no clear answers, she started rubbing her temples. There it was again. A deep ache settled in her head.

It happened every time. Every damn time she had a dream like this. A sharp throb as if something was pushing against her head. What if these dreams are more than just dreams? Sometimes, it felt like she was losing track of reality. But was she?

She had always been different from the other girls. While her friends would run off to play, laughing and chasing each other, Layla preferred solitude. She'd head to the shade of a massive oak tree near her school and rest there. The quiet gave her a sense of peace that the chaos of the playground never did.

And when it came to the things her classmates cared about—like the latest hairstyles—Layla couldn't have cared less. She had long, dark hair that reached almost to her hips. While others were cutting their hair into trendy styles, she kept hers simple. Braided neatly every day for school, it was a style that suited her calm, unhurried nature.

With her long braids and the soft, innocent expression on her face, Layla stood out—but in a quiet, beautiful way. Different, yes, but not in a way that made her feel out of place. It was just who she was.

She let out a soft sigh and glanced toward the window. What if these dreams were a sign? A way of telling her she needed to go out more, have fun, maybe spend time with her friends? She imagined herself at the park, laughing with her classmates, or at the mall, trying on silly outfits just for fun. But as soon as the thought came, an invisible weight seemed to settle on her shoulders.

Her body felt heavy sluggish, like it didn't want her to move, didn't want her to leave her comfort zone. The idea of being surrounded by people made her chest tighten. It wasn't fear exactly, but something else—something deeper, harder to explain. Maybe she was meant to be alone, to find peace in the stillness of her own company.

Layla's gaze shifted to the bed. Her mother lay fast asleep; her chest was rising and falling in the soft rhythm of dreams. Layla envied her, the way sleep seemed to come so easily to her mother. For Layla, sleep often brought more questions than rest.

The house was quiet, unusually so. Her father was out of town on business, and as an only child, Layla had grown used to the stillness. But tonight, it felt different. The silence pressed in around her like it was hiding something just out of sight.

Then she heard it—a knock.

It wasn't loud, just a soft, steady tapping that broke through the quiet. Layla froze, and her ears strained to catch the sound again. There it was. It wasn't coming from the bedroom door but somewhere further away.

Her heart quickened as she got up. She reached for the doorknob and pulled the door open slowly to peer into the hallway.

The hallway ahead was as dark as night, and she couldn't see anyone.

The knocking continued, faint but insistent. It seemed to echo from somewhere deeper in the house as if it was calling her. She stepped into the hallway, making the floorboards creak under her weight.

With each step, the air grew colder. The sound seemed to be coming from everywhere and nowhere all at once. Her fingers brushed against the walls to guide her in the dark as she moved forwards.

Her foot suddenly caught on something. It was small, hard, and completely unseen in the dim light. She stumbled forward and tried to catch her balance, but it was too late. Her head slammed into the wall with a sharp, jarring thud.

Pain exploded in her skull, sharp and blinding. She crumpled to the floor, her hands instinctively reaching for her head. The knocking sound grew softer, fading into the background until it disappeared completely.

The world around her blurred, the shadows twisting and shifting. Her breaths came in shallow gasps as the pain dulled into a strange, hollow ache. And then, as if someone had flipped a switch, everything went black.

***

The first thing Layla noticed was the beeping. It was soft, rhythmic, almost soothing in a strange way. Her head throbbed with a dull, steady ache, but she didn't open her eyes yet. The light beyond her eyelids felt too bright, too harsh like it would make the pain worse if she tried to face it.

She lay still, listening. Faint voices drifted toward her, hushed and serious. One voice belonged to her mother—Layla recognized the slight tremor in it. Her mother always sounded like that when she was worried. Her father was speaking too, his tone low and steady, as though trying to reassure someone.

But there was another voice, unfamiliar. A man's voice. Calm, measured, and warm, with a slight accent that hinted at wisdom and experience. Layla listened intently to focus on the words.

"We've taken her to doctors," her father was saying. "They've done scans, tests... but everything comes back normal. They say there's nothing wrong with her."

"I understand," the unfamiliar voice replied. "These matters are not always physical. Sometimes, they go beyond what medicine can explain."

Her mother's voice broke in, trembling. "We don't know what to do anymore, Imam Farid. She's been having these strange dreams, hearing things... acting distant. It's like she's not even our Layla anymore."

Layla's heart skipped a beat. They thought something was wrong with her?

The man, Imam Farid, spoke again. "These symptoms you've described—dreams, voices, feelings of heaviness—they are not uncommon in cases of possession. But we must approach this carefully, with faith and patience. May I assess her?"

Her father hesitated. "Will it hurt her?"

"Not at all," the imam assured them. "She may feel a little discomfort, but I promise it will not harm her. We are only seeking the truth of what she is experiencing."

Layla's pulse quickened. Possession? What were they talking about?

She heard soft footsteps approaching her bed. The warmth of a hand rested gently on her forehead, and a faint scent of musk filled the air. The man's voice became softer, more focused, as though he were speaking not to her parents but to something else entirely.

"In the name of Allah, the Most Gracious, the Most Merciful," he murmured. Layla recognised those words, but she didn't entirely know what they meant. Yet, they brought comfort to her.

The imam continued to speak, and the sense of comfort she had been feeling mere moments before was replaced by a strange sensation. It rippled through her body. It wasn't pain exactly, but unease. It felt like something within her body was being pulled to the surface.

Suddenly, her fingers started twitching. Next, she could hear a low hum drowning out all the external noise.

Then it came.

A voice—not hers, not the imam's—played in her mind. It was deep and guttural. It spoke in a language she couldn't understand. Layla's breathing quickened, and she felt her body stiffen against her will.

"She's reacting," the imam said calmly. "This confirms what I suspected."

"What is it?" her mother asked, her voice breaking.

The imam paused, his tone grave but steady. "Your daughter is not sick. She is being influenced by a Jinn."

A gasp escaped Layla's mother, and her father swore under his breath.

The imam continued, "This is not something to fear, but it is serious. Jinn are beings created by Allah, like humans, but made of smokeless fire. They can influence or possess people for many reasons—sometimes out of anger, sometimes out of mischief. But with Allah's help, we can free her."

Tears streamed down her mother's face as she whispered, "Can she... can she go back to being herself?"

"InshaAllah," the imam replied with conviction. "We will begin the process to help her, but it will take time, prayer, and faith. She is strong, and so are you."

As Layla lay there, her eyes still closed, her heart raced. What did this mean for her? What was inside her? She had so many questions but no strength to voice them. For now, all she could do was listen, hope, and hold on.

Imam Farid adjusted the chair beside Layla's bed and sat close to her. His voice carried a calm authority as he explained, "The first step is to invoke Allah's name and recite verses from the Qur'an. These are words of protection and guidance. With His permission, the Jinn will have no choice but to leave."

Layla's parents exchanged worried glances but nodded. Her mother clasped her hands tightly, her knuckles white, while her father stood rigid, his face etched with concern.

Imam Farid placed his hand gently on Layla's head again, murmuring softly, "Layla, if you can hear me, stay calm. You are not alone. We are here with you, and Allah is with you."

Layla wanted to respond, to tell them she was listening, but her body refused to cooperate. Her limbs felt heavy, as though something unseen was holding her down.

The imam began reciting verses from the Qur'an in a steady, melodic tone. "Bismillah-ir-Rahman-ir-Raheem," he started. He recited Surah Al-Falaq and Surah An-Nas, verses often used to seek refuge from harm and evil.

As the words filled the room, Layla felt a strange sensation stirring within her—a pressure building in her chest, like a balloon being inflated too far. Her breathing quickened, and her fingers curled into fists against her will.

The imam continued, even as Layla's body began to tremble. "A'udhu billahi min ash-shaytan-ir-rajim," he said, seeking protection from Satan and his followers. He placed his other hand lightly on her shoulder, steadying her.

Layla's mother sobbed quietly, whispering prayers under her breath. Her father gripped her mother's shoulder.

Suddenly, a guttural growl escaped Layla's lips—a sound that didn't belong to her. Her eyes snapped open, but they didn't look like hers. They were darker, almost black, with an intensity that made her parents recoil.

The imam didn't falter. "By the will of Allah, leave her," he commanded firmly. He recited Ayat-ul-Kursi, a powerful verse from the Qur'an known for its protective qualities.

The growling grew louder, and Layla's body arched slightly off the bed, as though something inside her was resisting. Her breaths came in shallow gasps, and beads of sweat formed on her forehead.

"Layla," the imam said, addressing her directly. "You are stronger than this. You are under Allah's protection. Stay with us."

Layla's vision blurred, and a sharp pain shot through her head, like a thousand needles pressing into her skull. The pressure in her chest became unbearable, and she let out a piercing scream.

Then, as abruptly as it started, everything stopped. Her body went limp, her head falling to the side. The room fell silent except for the beeping of the machines and the faint sound of her mother's cries.

"She's unconscious," her father said, his voice thick with panic. "Is she okay?"

Imam Farid wiped his forehead, his voice calm but firm. "This is normal. The Jinn is resisting but losing its hold. She is in Allah's hands now. We must continue the prayers."

He motioned for Layla's parents to join him in prayer, and together, they recited Surah Al-Baqarah, a chapter known to repel evil forces. As the verses filled the room, a faint chill seemed to lift, replaced by a sense of peace.

Layla lay still, her chest rising and falling in shallow breaths. Though unconscious, her face looked calmer, as though a weight had been lifted. But the imam knew the battle wasn't over yet.

"We'll continue this process," he said softly, turning to her parents. "With Allah's help, she will heal. Trust in Him and remain steadfast."

Her parents nodded. They sat beside their daughter, their hands clasped tightly, whispering prayers into the quiet of the room as the imam prepared for the next step.

Chapter 2: The Forgotten Prophecy

September 8, 2014

People say that what slips from memory doesn't always vanish; it waits, hidden, for the right time to return. Some may not believe it until it happens to them.

It had been ten years since Layla's exorcism. To the world, she seemed perfectly normal. She smiled at neighbours, attended family gatherings, and spoke of mundane things like weather and groceries. Healthy, even. But inside, in the quiet corners of her soul, Layla concealed a secret she couldn't share.

The night of the exorcism had been seared into her family's memory. It wasn't the kind of thing anyone could forget. When the Imam had finished his prayers, his expression remained uncertain. He wiped the sweat from his brow, looked at Layla's parents, and said, "I cannot say for sure if the Jinn is gone. We will only know when she wakes."

And so, they waited. Layla lay unconscious with shallow yet steady breathing. Her mother sat by the bedside, clutching a rosary, whispering prayers under her breath. Her father paced the small hospital room with trembling hands while he pretended to scroll through his phone. They grew more anxious and impatient with every passing hour.

Twenty-four hours passed before the doctors allowed her to be discharged. They could find no medical reason to keep her. "Rest," they said. "It's all she needs." An ambulance brought her home, and the family set her up in her childhood bedroom.

Then, one evening, Layla stirred. Her eyes fluttered open, unfocused and glassy at first. Her mother leaned in.

"Water," Layla whispered. Her voice was dry and cracked, as though it had come from somewhere far away.

Her parents exhaled together and instantly released the tension of a thousand prayers. But as they rushed to fulfil her simple request, Layla's mind began to work—slowly, carefully. Memories of that night, the prayers, the struggle, and the dark, suffocating presence all hovered at the edges of her consciousness, just out of reach. Something remained, watching, waiting.

Even as she drank, Layla felt it—the faintest shadow in her chest, like an echo.

And it wasn't gone. Not entirely.

As the days passed, Layla's strength returned. At first, she could barely sit up in bed. Her mother fed her soups and whispered prayers under her breath. Her father brought fresh flowers to brighten the room. Slowly, Layla regained her appetite and colour. The dark circles under her eyes faded, and she began to walk unsteadily through the house, leaning against walls for support.

Her family was relieved. The heavy silence that had enveloped their home for so long began to lift. The haunting cries, the late-night prayers, and the Imam's visits were becoming memories—ones they avoided speaking about. It was as if they all agreed, without saying it, that moving forward was the only way to forget.

Layla herself seemed to thrive physically. Her cheeks regained their rosy shade, her appetite grew heartier, and she even walked into the garden one afternoon to soak in the sunlight as if she were rediscovering it. Neighbours commented on how healthy she looked now, how normal. But Layla knew that what lay beneath her skin was far from normal.

At first, her memories of the possession clung to her like shadows. She remembered the screams that didn't sound like her own. The moments where her body felt like a puppet, controlled by invisible strings. The voices—some soft, some angry—that filled her mind.

But as the weeks turned into months, these memories began to blur, as if someone was carefully erasing them from her mind. The specific details slipped away, leaving only fragments. She couldn't remember the words of the prayers the Imam had recited or the exact feeling of the Jinn's presence.

Instead, one memory stayed sharp and clear, refusing to fade.

It was a voice—not hers, not the Imam's, not her parents'. It was something otherworldly.

"You will marry a prince."

The words kept replaying in her mind like a mantra, especially in the quiet hours of the night. It was strange. At first, she dismissed it as part of the hallucinations she must have experienced when she was unwell. But no matter how much she tried to brush it aside, the prophecy remained.

Layla didn't understand why this single detail stood out when everything else was dissolving into the fog of her mind. She told no one about it, not her mother, not the Imam, not even her closest friends. How could she explain it without sounding mad?

Physically, Layla was better than ever. She helped her mother with chores around the house, laughing and joking as they prepared meals. She walked to the market with her father, carrying bags of fruit and chatting about mundane things.

But her heart was restless.

Every night, when the house fell silent and her parents went to bed, Layla lay awake staring at the ceiling. The darkness pressed in around her, and the words of the prophecy would come back like a whisper.

"You will marry a prince."

At first, she tried to distract herself. She took up sewing, spent hours reading novels, and even began drawing, sketching flowers and landscapes in the margins of her notebooks. But nothing filled the void. A strange longing grew inside her—a pull toward something she couldn't name or understand.

By day, she felt trapped in the routines of normal life, suffocated by the smallness of her world. The market, the kitchen, the garden—these places felt too ordinary, too plain. At night, her dreams took her to unfamiliar places: grand palaces with golden halls, endless deserts beneath starry skies, and deep forests where shadows danced.

One evening, as Layla sat in the garden watching the sunset, a faint wind stirred the leaves. It was warm and carried a strange scent—something sweet and earthy, like jasmine mixed with rain.

A chill ran down her spine, though the air was far from cold.

"Layla," the wind seemed to whisper.

She sat up, her breath hitching. For a moment, she thought she had imagined it. But then it came again, faint but unmistakable.

"Layla."

She looked around, but the garden was empty. Her mother was inside preparing dinner, and her father was reading in the living room.

"Is someone there?" she called, her voice trembling.

The only answer was the rustling of leaves.

That night, she lay awake, her thoughts churning. Had she really heard her name, or was it her imagination? Was it connected to the prophecy?

She couldn't shake the feeling that something—someone—was watching her.

Over the weeks, the strange occurrences continued. A shadow flickering just at the edge of her vision. The sound of soft footsteps when she was alone. Objects slightly out of place, as if someone had touched them when she wasn't looking.

Each time it happened, her mind raced back to the prophecy.

"You will marry a prince."

It wasn't just a prediction anymore—it felt like a promise, one she couldn't ignore. But who was this prince? Where would she find him? And what did it all mean?

Layla began to obsess over the idea. She scoured the books in her father's study, looking for stories of prophecies and princes, of destiny and fate. She read ancient texts, fairy tales, and even religious scriptures, searching for answers.

Her friends noticed the change in her. "You're distracted," they said. "Are you feeling all right?"

Layla forced a smile and waved away their concerns. "I'm fine," she lied.

But she wasn't fine. The restlessness inside her grew stronger with each passing day, a gnawing ache that wouldn't let her be.

One night, Layla stood by her window, staring up at the full moon. It was bigger than usual, glowing softly against the dark sky. But something about it felt... different. As she looked closer, the patterns on its surface seemed to shift, forming the outline of a face. A sad, weary face. It almost looked like it was crying.

Layla swallowed hard, her chest tightening. Was she imagining things? Or was the universe trying to tell her something? Either way, she felt it deep in her bones—she couldn't stay here any longer. She couldn't keep waiting in this house, in this tiny town, hoping for answers that would never come. If the prophecy was real, she had to find the prince herself. And if it wasn't... she needed help before she lost herself completely.

She didn't know where to start, but something deep inside her whispered that she would know the way when the time came.

The next morning, Layla woke up determined to unravel the mystery that had been haunting her. After breakfast, she told her parents she was going to the library. Her mother smiled, pleased to see her taking interest in something again.

"Find something good to read," said her mother.

Layla nodded and left, clutching her notebook.

The library was a quiet haven, with rows of tall shelves lined with books of every kind. The faint scent of paper and ink filled the air. Layla approached the librarian, an elderly woman with kind eyes and a soft voice. "I'm looking for books about prophecies," she said hesitantly.

The librarian's brow furrowed. "Prophecies? That's a bit specific, but let me see what we have." She disappeared behind the counter and returned a few minutes later with a stack of books.

Layla thanked her and found a corner to sit in.

She spent hours flipping through the pages, reading about ancient seers, mystical predictions, and cryptic messages that shaped the fates of kings and empires. Some prophecies were tied to celestial events, others to visions or dreams. One book described how prophecies often carried dual meanings—one literal and one symbolic—making them nearly impossible to interpret until they unfolded.

Despite the intriguing stories, none of it felt personal or connected to her. Layla sighed in frustration, running her fingers through her hair.

When the library closed, she decided to turn to the internet. Back home, she opened her laptop and began typing furiously.

"What do prophecies m ean?"

"Can a prophecy come true?"

"Voices in dreams."

The results were overwhelming. Blog posts, forums, and videos popped up, filled with wild theories and personal anecdotes. One forum claimed that prophecies were often warnings meant to prepare people for challenges ahead. Another article suggested that prophecies were born from the subconscious mind, reflecting hidden desires or fears.

Nothing she found felt like the answer she was searching for. She leaned back in her chair, staring at the ceiling. Was she chasing something that didn't exist?

As the days passed, Layla began to feel drained. The obsession with the prophecy was consuming her. It was leaving her restless and unsettled. She started to wonder if the voice had been a trick of her mind.

But how could she let it go?

One evening, while browsing online, she stumbled across an article about **Avicenna**, a renowned Persian physician and philosopher. It mentioned his work titled **"The Medicines of the Heart"**—a collection of teachings meant to heal not just the body but the mind and soul.

The words struck a chord in Layla. For the first time in weeks, she felt a flicker of hope.

Layla spent hours researching Avicenna and his philosophies. Known as Ibn Sina in the Islamic world, Avicenna was one of the most brilliant minds of the medieval era. His works spanned medicine, philosophy, and metaphysics, and he believed that the health of the heart was deeply tied to the health of the soul.

"Medicines of the Heart" wasn't just a book about curing ailments. It was a guide to achieving inner peace and balance. Avicenna wrote about emotions like fear, anger, and sorrow, describing how they could affect the body if left unchecked. He believed that the heart was the seat of the soul, and if one needs to lead a harmonious life, one need to nurture the heart.

Layla was captivated. One passage, in particular, stood out to her:

"The restless heart seeks answers not outside but within. The cure is not in the stars, nor in the words of men, but in the stillness of one's own soul."

The words felt like they were written just for her.

Determined to put Avicenna's teachings into practice, Layla began her journey of self-healing.

First, she started with solitude. Every morning, before the world stirred awake, she sat in the garden, listening to the birds and the rustling of leaves. She practised deep breathing, letting the cool morning air fill her lungs and clear her mind.

Next, she focused on gratitude. Each night before bed, she wrote down three things she was thankful for, no matter how small—her mother's laughter, the warmth of the sun, the taste of fresh fruit.

But despite her efforts, no matter what she did, the relief she felt was always temporary. Each time Layla thought she was making progress, her mind would slowly drift back to that voice—the prophecy. It wouldn't let her go. It was like trying to chase away a shadow that always returned when the light faded.

The more she practised Avicenna's teachings, the more she realised something unsettling. The peace she felt was fragile. At first, it seemed like a breakthrough. Her heart felt lighter, and she felt calmer. She had moments where she believed the prophecy no longer held its power over her. But sooner or later, that feeling would fade. The restless heart she was trying to heal always seemed to return like a tide that would never stay still.

The prophecy, once a whisper in the back of her mind, slowly began to grow louder again. *You will marry a prince*. The words seemed to cling to her. What did it mean? Why couldn't she just forget about it?

Frustration began to build up in her chest. No matter how hard she tried, the sense of restlessness would return. It would always leave her feeling lost once more. The silence and solitude she'd been practising didn't feel enough anymore. She needed something more—something tangible to help her break free from this cycle.

One afternoon, while sitting in her room, trying to meditate in the quiet, Layla's thoughts wandered back to her childhood. She remembered stories her grandmother used to tell her, stories about the power of food and herbs from faraway lands. Her grandmother had always believed that the food you ate could heal your body, mind, and soul.

There was something about the way her grandmother spoke of food. She didn't just talk about nutrition but about the spirit of the food, the cultures, and the traditions that shaped it. Layla wondered if, perhaps, the right foods could help her heal—like the missing piece of the puzzle.

Determined to find something, Layla began researching. She learned about ancient healing foods from all over the world—ingredients that had been used for centuries to restore balance and peace. There were foods from India, China, the Middle East, and even the deep jungles of South America. All of them were linked by one idea: food could heal more than just the body.

Layla was determined to find something that would bring her lasting peace, something that would help her break free from the cycle of temporary relief. But she knew she couldn't just leave her home and search for healing foods from distant lands like someone on a grand adventure. Living with her parents, she was bound by the customs and routines of her family. Yet, Layla was clever and resourceful. She decided to use the resources she had available—research, local stores, and the internet.

She searched the internet for anything that might offer a solution, reading articles and watching videos on natural healing. Her fascination grew as she came across countless remedies from cultures far and wide. Layla decided to start with the foods she could find locally, items that were easily accessible through local markets and online shops.

Her first attempt took her to **turmeric**, an ancient spice known for its healing properties, particularly its ability to calm inflammation and bring clarity. She had heard about it in various articles, especially for its role in mental and emotional wellness. Layla asked her mother if she could visit the local market, and her mother gladly agreed, thinking it was part of Layla's interest in healthy living.

At the market, Layla found turmeric powder in a small glass jar. She carefully examined the label, reading about its long history in Ayurvedic medicine as a natural remedy for the mind and body. She picked up a jar of ground turmeric and headed home, eager to try it for herself.

At home, she made a simple **turmeric latte**—a mixture of turmeric powder, warm milk, and honey. She had heard it was soothing and could help promote mental clarity. As she sipped the golden drink, a sense of comfort washed over her. The warmth of the milk, combined with the earthy taste of the turmeric and the sweetness of the honey, brought a temporary peace to her soul. For a few hours, she felt at ease, her mind free of the heavy thoughts. For a brief moment, it felt like she had found the answer to her restless heart. But as the day went on, that sense of peace began to fade, and once again, the prophecy echoed in her mind. The relief was only temporary.

Refusing to give up, Layla moved on to her next remedy. This time, she turned to **ginseng**, a root widely used in traditional Chinese medicine for its ability to restore energy and balance. She found a small box of ginseng tea at a nearby herbal shop. Layla had heard that ginseng was known to help those who felt mentally drained and disconnected, and she was hopeful it might offer a solution.

She brewed a pot of the tea and let the scent fill the room. As she sipped the tea, she could feel a sense of alertness wash over her. Her mind, which had been clouded by the heavy thoughts of the prophecy, felt clearer. For a moment, it seemed like the ginseng was working. The fog in her thoughts lifted, and her heart felt less burdened.

But as before, after a few hours, the restlessness crept back in. The sense of peace that ginseng had briefly given her faded as she was once again confronted with the weight of the prophecy.

Not one to give up, Layla turned her attention to her own heritage and looked for **Middle Eastern remedies** that had been passed down through generations. One such remedy she found was **rose water**. Rose water was believed to have a soothing effect on the spirit, bringing peace and balance to the heart.

Layla had used rose water in desserts as a child, but now she saw it in a new light. She decided to add a few drops of rose water to her tea, just as she had seen in some recipes online. As she sipped, the floral scent filled her senses, and for a moment, her heart felt lighter. It was a gentle, soothing feeling, like the soft petals of a flower caressing her soul. She closed her eyes and breathed deeply, savouring the moment.

But, as with the other remedies, the relief didn't last. The shadows of the prophecy slowly returned, clouding her mind once more.

Layla's frustration only grew with time. She soon realised it didn't matter what she ate or sought; the peace she was looking for couldn't be found in external things.

Every time she tried something promising, it would only bring temporary relief. Perhaps it was because the source of her unrest wasn't a physical illness. Maybe it was something deeper. Maybe it's her heart and mind that's unwell. She needed to stop holding onto the prophecy.

But how? Layla thought about it for weeks until it finally hit her. She has been trying to outrun it all along. She has only considered it a burden that needs to be escaped.

What if she tried a different approach? An approach that doesn't involve her avoiding the prophecy. What if she embraced it instead? Maybe the answer is to understand it rather than fight it.

She closed her eyes, letting the quiet settle around her. She had spent so much time trying to find the perfect food, the perfect remedy, the perfect way to silence the restless voice in her mind. But what if the answer wasn't in food at all? What if it was about accepting herself, accepting the prophecy, and letting go of the fear that had grown around it?

But even as the thought began to take root, Layla felt a stir of unease deep within her. What would it mean for her life if she let go of that fear? Would she finally feel free? Or would something else, something even more unsettling, take its place?

Layla felt a sudden chill run through her. Her thoughts were swirling like a storm. She couldn't explain it, but something told her this was the beginning of something important—something that would change everything.

She couldn't shake the feeling that this was just the start.

Chapter 3: The Vision

Layla hoped that if she stopped running from the prophecy, it would finally leave her alone. Maybe she'd feel normal again. Maybe the nightmares would stop, and she could get her life back. Just maybe, things would go back to how they used to be.

Little did she know, it doesn't work like that. You can hope all you want, but in the end, fate always has the final say.

Layla had stopped thinking about the prophecy – or at least she tried to. She didn't let it consume her anymore. She stopped searching for answers. She believed that if it was meant to be, the answers would come to her. But they didn't. And nothing got better. Instead, things started to take a turn for the worse.

On the night of the blood moon, Layla's eyes rolled back to the point that one could only see the white. Her weak, petite body started to tremble.

She saw herself standing under a sky where stars moved like flowing water, shifting and reshaping into patterns that spoke of destiny. The constellations revealed two figures: one crowned in starlight and the other—Layla herself—wrapped in silver mist from the spirit world.

The moon shattered into seven pieces, and each piece glowed with a different colour. Within those magical hues, she saw glimpses of her future.

- In the red light, she saw herself wearing royal robes.
- In the gold, a crown was being placed on her head.

- In the white, a wedding took place in a palace of marble and jade.
- In the blue, she held children with eyes that glowed like hers.
- In the green, she stood in a peaceful garden.
- In the purple, her name sparkled among the stars.
- In the silver, her descendants carried the gift of second sight.

She saw herself flying over cities of brass and crystal, where mechanical birds delivered messages between tall towers. She walked through gardens where flowers burned with flames instead of petals and fountains poured streams of glowing starlight.

In the clearest vision, she stood on the highest tower of a palace made of moonlight. Beside her was a figure whose face was hidden by shifting constellations. This was the prince tied to her fate. When he looked at her, his eyes gleamed with an unearthly light Layla couldn't quite put a finger on. The vision ended with a wedding, where the stars themselves came down to dance around them. When the vision finally released her, Layla collapsed.

It was the same every time. Whenever the visions ended, real life was hard. Layla would shake for hours afterward, and her skin would give off a faint glow that took days to fade. She would find sparkly footprints behind her when she walked, and sometimes, when she spoke, her voice sounded ancient and wise in a way that scared people.

This became her reality. The visions would come without warning, filling Layla's mind with images of the prophecy. They left her shaken, her nights sleepless, and her days haunted by the feeling that something beyond her control was drawing closer. She tried to push them away, to pretend they weren't real, but the memories never left her alone. Not even for a second.

It wasn't long before the news of Layla's strange experiences spread through the small town. The whispers started quietly at first, but soon, they grew louder and reached every corner of the community. Some people claimed that the Jinn still possessed her, refusing to leave her body. Others believed she was being punished for some terrible sins, sins too grave to be forgiven.

Parents began warning their daughters to stay away from Layla. They feared that her supposed curse might spread to them. Friends who used to once share their secrets and jokes with Layla now avoided her completely. They would cross the street if they ever saw her in the market, so they don't have to stop by even for small talk.

With each passing day, Layla felt lonelier than ever. It wasn't that she was alone—she was always surrounded by people. Yet, somehow, she had never felt more isolated. No one truly saw her. No one truly understood.

Except for the moon.

Night after night, she found herself looking up at it, the only constant in a world that felt like it was slipping away from her. Its soft glow was the closest thing to comfort she had. But lately, the moon cotinued to seem sad. As if it, too, carried a weight too heavy to bear. Its craters looked like tired eyes, its glow dimmer than before. And on some nights, she swore she could see tears slipping down its face.

Maybe she was imagining it. Or maybe the universe was trying to tell her something.

Either way, the emptiness inside her was growing.

As for her parents, they were desperate to marry her off. They believed marriage might bring a sense of normalcy to her life again. They tried speaking to matchmakers, visited families, and convinced anyone who would listen that their daughter was completely alright. But all their attempts proved futile. Every suitable bachelor in the city kept his distance from Layla. The rumours about her possession and punishment were too strong. No one wanted to get caught in its crosshairs.

Layla felt the weight of it all. She saw her parents' desperation. She witnessed the town's judgment. And the prophecy? It wouldn't let her go. She wondered if there was any way out of this life if there was a future where she could be free of the visions and the whispers. But for now, all she could do was endure.

Layla would sit by her window every night and look up at the stars that haunted her dreams. She couldn't help but wonder if the prophecy was a curse or a blessing. Granted, it promised her a prince and a wonderful future. But right now, it was making everything so difficult. She felt stuck between two worlds. On one hand, there's the normal life she once used to have. On the other, there was this strange new life that filled her with hope for a magical future.

Sometimes, she would catch her reflection in a mirror and see a faint glow in her eyes, reminding her that she was different now. Forever changed by Jinn's prophecy, Layla waited for the day when all these visions would make sense, trying to stay strong even when it felt like the whole town had turned against her.

The more Layla tried to make sense of what was happening to her, the stronger her heart pulled her toward the mausoleum of

Avicenna. It was an unexplainable feeling as if some invisible force was guiding her there. She didn't know why she felt this way, but the desire grew stronger with every passing day. The mausoleum seemed to hold an answer, or at least the possibility of relief from the turmoil inside her.

But visiting the place was no simple task. The mausoleum of Avicenna was more than three hours away from her town. It wasn't a journey she could make alone. How would she leave the home for such a long time without getting her parents' permission? It was out of the question. The only possible option was to convince them and gain their trust. But how could Layla explain this strange calling when she herself didn't quite understand it?

Layla thought about it for days. Then, she decided to approach her parents because that was the only way. If she didn't ask, the answer would forever remain no. So, she prepared a speech in her mind before she sat down before them one afternoon.

Trying to ignore her racing heartbeat, Layla started the conversation. "Mama, Baba... I think I know a cure to my condition."

Her parents looked at each other. None of them knew what Layla was going to say next, but they were sure about one thing: if there was even the slightest chance that something could help their daughter, they were ready to take the chances.

"Go ahead, dear," her father gently asked. "What do you think it is?"

Layla inhaled deeply. "Baba, I wish to visit the mausoleum of Avicenna. I'm not sure why, but I have this feeling that my remedy lies there."

For a brief moment, her parents said nothing. They just stared at her while they struggled to process Layla's request. They certainly wanted their daughter to be well again, yet they couldn't understand what was drawing her to the mausoleum.

After a moment of contemplation, her father leaned back. "The mausoleum of Avicenna is far from here, my dear. Are you sure it will help you?"

"I don't know, Baba. But I'll never find out if I don't go there." Layla firmly replied.

Her mother reached out and placed a hand on Layla's arm. She looked at her husband, Layla's father, for his approval. Once he nodded, she said, "If this is what you think can help, allow us time to think about it. We will have to plan the journey, my dear."

Layla felt a sense of relief was over her. This small conversation with her parents felt like a step closer to the journey she may be destined to take.

In the following days, the family was consumed by hushed discussions and planning for the trip. Layla's parents, although hesitant, knew this trip deeply mattered to their daughter. So, they decided Layla's mother would accompany her. Letting Layla visit the mausoleum all alone wasn't an option. It wasn't safe.

The next morning, just as the sun began to rise, Layla and her mother set off in their small car towards their destination. The journey was long and quiet. Layla didn't speak a word throughout the ride; she just quietly stared out the window.

Her mind was swirling with hope and fear. What if this trip didn't help? What if she left the mausoleum feeling the same, or worse, more lost than ever? She clutched her scarf tightly, trying to calm her racing thoughts.

Her mother glanced at her occasionally. "We'll get there soon," she said gently. Layla nodded, her lips pressed into a tight line.

By the time they arrived at the mausoleum, the sun was high in the sky. The mausoleum was tall and majestic, just like Layla had seen in the pictures. The walls were adorned with intricate patterns carved by hands that had worked centuries ago.

Layla felt a strange calm wash over her as she stepped out of the car. The air here felt different—thicker, charged, as if the place held centuries of secrets waiting to be discovered. Her mother walked beside her up the steps, holding her hand for support.

At the grand wooden doors of the mausoleum, her mother stopped. "Go on, Layla. I'll wait out here," she said. Layla hesitated for a moment, then nodded and pushed the heavy door open.

Inside, the mausoleum was cool and dimly lit, with shafts of sunlight streaming through small, stained-glass windows. The walls were covered in inscriptions—verses of poetry, fragments of ancient wisdom, and lines from Avicenna's works.

Layla paused before a large plaque inscribed with an excerpt from Avicenna's writings. Her fingers traced the letters as she read aloud, "The mind sees beyond the veil of the present. Prophecies are not chains; they are whispers of possibility."

She felt a flutter in her chest. Is this a clue? Was she wrong all along to think that her prophecy was a fixed destiny? Maybe it was merely a guide to choices she doesn't yet understand. Just then, her eyes landed on a small alcove to the right of the room. She noticed an open book on the pedestal and felt drawn to it.

Approaching cautiously, she realised the book was filled with dense script. Its pages were fragile and yellowed with age. One passage caught her eye:

"The bearer of visions carries both burden and power. To seek answers, they must first seek understanding of the self."

The words sent a shiver down her spine. Was this what she had been missing all along—understanding herself?

Lost in thought, she barely noticed the soft sound of footsteps approaching. She turned abruptly only to find herself face to face with a stranger. He was tall and lean, with a quiet presence that seemed almost otherworldly. His dark eyes met hers as though he could see straight into her soul.

"You've come seeking answers," he said in a low and steady voice.

Layla froze. "Who are you?" she managed to whisper.

The man gave a small, enigmatic smile. "Someone who knows the weight of what you carry. And someone who knows where your journey leads."

Before Layla could respond, the faint sound of her mother calling her name came from outside. The man's expression darkened slightly as though he knew their time was up.

"We'll meet again," he said, stepping back into the shadows.

Layla blinked, and he was gone. She stood there, her heart racing, trying to process what had just happened. What did he mean? Who was he? And why did it feel like this was just the beginning of something much bigger?

Chapter 4: The Stranger

A few days had passed since Layla visited the mausoleum of Avicenna. When she went there, she had a heart full of hope. She firmly believed that the trip would bring her the peace and clarity she so desperately wanted. But now, as time went by, she was only growing more frustrated with her condition.

The recovery she was craving was nowhere to be found. Her nights were still restless. Her mind was still foggy. And the prophecy? Oh, it stayed at the top of her mind regardless of how hard she tried to push it away.

And then, there was that man.

For some reason, Layla couldn't stop thinking about the stranger she had bumped into her at the mausoleum. It was like an imprint on her mind that wouldn't fade. Somehow, it made things worse.

Before the trip, it was just the prophecy that troubled her. But now, her mind was split between the chilling words of the prophecy and the unsettling mystery of this man. Who was he? Why had he approached her? And what did he mean by, *"We will meet again?"*

The questions circled endlessly in her mind. Questions that had no answer. She was growing weary. It felt as if life itself was toying with her. As if it was weaving an inescapable web of riddles. The hope she had held onto was slipping through her fingers. Maybe this was her fate—to live in isolation, burdened by the prophecy, destined to endure the weight of it alone.

And then, one fine afternoon, something happened that would shift everything.

It was an ordinary day, quiet and uneventful. Layla's father was at work, and she was alone in the house with her mother. Her mother was working in the kitchen, cooking her favourite lentil soup. Layla, lost in her own thoughts, was sitting in the living room staring blankly out the window.

The sharp sound of the doorbell broke through the stillness.

"Layla, could you see who it is?" her mother called out.

Layla sighed and dragged herself out of her trance. She didn't particularly feel like answering the door, but she got up reluctantly.

When she opened the door, she froze.

A stranger stood there, holding a large cardboard box in his hands. He was young, maybe in his late twenties, with a calm yet unnerving presence. His deep-set eyes locked onto hers, and for a moment, she felt as though he could see right through her. His face was serious, though not unkind, and his simple attire gave nothing away about who he might be.

"Layla?" he said.

Her stomach twisted. "Yes… that's me. Who are you?"

The man shifted the box slightly as if to adjust its weight in his hands. "I was asked to deliver this to you."

Layla's heart thudded. "By whom?"

The man hesitated. "You'll know soon enough," he said quietly and extended the box toward her.

She stared at it, unsure whether to take it or shut the door in his face. The box was plain and unmarked, but something about it felt… significant. Her hands trembled slightly as she reached out and took it.

"Wait," she said. "Are you… were you at the mausoleum of Avicenna?"

For a brief moment, his expression flickered—just a hint of something she couldn't quite place. Recognition? Regret? Whatever it was, it vanished as quickly as it appeared.

"You'll find what you're looking for," he said in a cryptic tone. Then, without another word, he turned and walked away. Layla just stood there in the doorway, holding the box. Her mind was spinning.

"Who was it, Layla?" her mother called from the kitchen. Her voice pulled Layla back to reality.

"I… I don't know," Layla replied, still staring down the empty street where the man had disappeared.

Her mother appeared behind her. "What's that you're holding?"

Layla stepped back inside and set the box on the dining table. "He said it was for me," she murmured.

"Well, open it. Let's see what's inside," her mother said.

Layla hesitated. Her fingers hovered over the tape, sealing the box momentarily. Then, slowly, she peeled it open to reveal its contents. Inside was a bundle wrapped in old, tattered cloth. She carefully unwrapped it to find three objects: an old journal, a small wooden box carved with intricate designs, and a sealed envelope with her name written on it in an elegant, flowing script.

It had been days since Layla's trip to the mausoleum of Avicenna, but the relief she was hoping for hadn't come. She felt no different, no lighter, no freer from the suffocating weight of the prophecy. It clung to her mind like a stubborn shadow, clouding her thoughts and tightening its grip on her soul.

And then there was the man—the stranger who had appeared so suddenly, then disappeared just as mysteriously. Before the mausoleum, it was only the prophecy that haunted her. But now, her thoughts were split. Who was he? Why did he speak to her like he knew her? And what did he mean by, "We will meet again?"

The questions circled endlessly in her mind, but no answers came. Frustration began to creep in, slowly turning into despair. Maybe she was foolish to believe there was a solution at all. Maybe the prophecy was just fate's way of telling her she was destined for solitude, for a life of unanswered questions.

She tried to push the thoughts aside, to go about her days as though nothing had happened. But just when she had almost given up—when she had started to convince herself that none of it mattered anymore—there came a knock at the door.

It was a sunny afternoon. Layla's father was at work, and her mother was in the kitchen, humming softly as she prepared lunch.

"Layla, could you see who it is?" her mother called out.

Reluctantly, Layla rose from the couch, her feet dragging slightly as she made her way to the door. She opened it, expecting to see a neighbour or maybe a delivery man.

Instead, a stranger stood there, holding a large cardboard box.

"Miss Layla?" the man asked, his voice calm but firm.

"Yes?" Layla replied cautiously, her eyes narrowing as she studied him. He was neatly dressed, with an air of professionalism, but there was something unusual about him—something she couldn't quite put her finger on.

"This is for you," he said, handing her the box.

"For me?" she echoed, confused.

"Yes. It's been sent by someone who wishes to remain anonymous. They said you would understand."

Before she could ask anything else, the man nodded politely, turned, and walked away, disappearing down the street.

Layla stared after him, the box heavy in her hands. What could this be? And who would send her something so cryptic?

"Who was it?" her mother asked, stepping into the room and wiping her hands on a dishcloth.

"I don't know," Layla murmured, setting the box down on the coffee table. "He just… gave me this."

Her mother looked just as puzzled as Layla felt. "Well, open it. Let's see what's inside."

With a deep breath, Layla lifted the lid of the box. The first thing she saw was an old journal, its leather cover cracked and worn with age. Beneath it was a small booklet, a dozen fresh figs carefully arranged in soft padding, and an envelope.

She picked up the journal first. Its weight in her hands felt significant, as though it carried something important within its pages. She opened it carefully.

The first page contained a verse that immediately caught her attention:

"I swear by the Fig and the Olive."

Her heart skipped a beat. It was a verse from the Quran—one she knew but had never given much thought to. She read on, and her eyes widened.

The journal described figs as the "Fruit of Heaven." It listed their health benefits in detail. They were said to cleanse the body, heal ailments, and restore balance to the soul. Each page seemed to whisper a quiet hope, as though the fruit held a secret far greater than she could imagine.

Her hands trembled slightly as she set the journal down and reached for the booklet. It was smaller but filled with illustrations and descriptions of figs—how they were rich in nutrients, good for digestion, and beneficial for mental clarity.

Then her gaze fell to the figs themselves. Their deep purple skins glistened in the sunlight, and their faint, sweet aroma filled the room. They looked perfect, almost too perfect, like something out of a dream.

Finally, she opened the envelope. The letter inside was brief, written in a handwriting that matched the journal.

"Layla,
The fruit before you is no ordinary gift. It is a remedy for the body and the soul. Trust its power. Trust yourself. Begin with one, and let it guide you. The answers will come.
— A Friend"

Layla read the letter twice, her mind racing. Who was this "friend"? And why figs? Could they really hold the key to her recovery?

"What does it say?" her mother asked gently.

Layla handed her the letter, her eyes still fixed on the figs. "I don't know, Mama. But… I think I have to eat them."

Her mother hesitated. "Layla, I don't like this. What if it's dangerous?"

"I'm not sure, Mama," Layla whispered. "But I think… I think it's connected to the prophecy."

Layla's mother carefully packed the figs back into the box and set it aside. "We don't know who sent them or why. What if they're poisoned or… or spoiled?"

"Mama," Layla tried to protest softly. She tried to explain the letter and the significance of the journal. But her mother wouldn't hear of it.

"I'm only looking out for you, Layla. You've been through enough already. I can't let you take that kind of risk."

And that was the end of it. The box was pushed into a cupboard, out of sight and out of reach. Layla didn't have the energy to argue. She simply nodded and walked away, though her heart ached with frustration.

That evening, Layla continually tried to distract herself. She sat on the couch with a book in her hands, but the words blurred together. Her mind continued to wander back to the figs. They were so fresh, so fragrant. How could something that smelled so sweet and earthy be poisonous or spoiled?

Her mother was wrong. She has to be. Those figs surely contained the remedy to her sickness. By the time night fell, the curiosity and longing had become too much to bear.

Layla lay in bed, staring at the ceiling. All she could hear was the sound of the refrigerator from the kitchen and the soft snores of her parents.

When she was sure everyone was asleep, she slipped out of bed. The hallway was dark, but she moved with purpose. It was as if her body was guided by a pull she couldn't explain.

In the kitchen, she opened the cupboard quietly. Her hands trembled slightly as she retrieved the box. The figs were just as she remembered—plump and perfect. Without hesitation, she took one and held it to her nose, inhaling its sweet aroma. Then, slowly, she bit into it.

The taste was even more magical than she had imagined. Sweet and rich, with a texture that melted in her mouth. She finished the fig quickly, then reached for another, and another, until she had eaten four.

As she stood there, a strange sensation washed over her. It wasn't dramatic—no sudden burst of energy or overwhelming emotion—but it was there, subtle and comforting.

For the first time in years, her chest didn't feel as heavy. The constant ache in her mind eased. It was replaced by a quiet calm.

Layla returned to her room. She climbed into bed, expecting her usual restlessness, but instead, sleep came quickly and easily.

That night, she dreamed of a huge garden filled with trees heavy with fruit. The air was warm and fragrant, and in the distance, she heard a soft voice calling her name.

When she woke the next morning, she felt different. Rested. Peaceful.

Her mother noticed the change almost immediately.

"You look better today," she said over breakfast, her eyes narrowing with suspicion. "Did something happen?"

"No, Mama," Layla replied, keeping her tone light. "I think I just slept well for once."

Her mother gave her a long, searching look but said nothing more.

A few days later, Layla was in the middle of tidying her room when the doorbell rang again.

"Layla, could you get that?" her father called from the living room.

Layla hesitated, her heart skipping a beat. She knew who it was before she even reached the door.

The same man stood there, holding another box. "This is for you," he said, just as he had before.

Layla nodded, taking the box without a word.

"Wait," she said as he turned to leave. "Who… who is sending these?"

The man paused, glancing at her with a small. "A kind Jewish man," he said simply.

Before she could ask more, he was gone.

This time, Layla didn't take the box to the kitchen. Instead, she carried it straight to her room, closing the door behind her.

Her fingers shook slightly as she opened it. Inside were several small bottles, each filled with a golden liquid that shimmered in the light. Fragrances, she realized. Essential oils, their labels handwritten with words like calm, clarity, and renewal.

At the bottom of the box was another letter. It was short, just like the first one:

"Layla,

These oils are meant to guide you further. Inhale deeply. Let them ground you. They will show you what you seek.

— A Friend"

Layla's heart raced as she read the note. Who was this friend? And how did he—or she—know so much about her struggles?

She tucked the box under her bed and hid it carefully. This time, she wouldn't tell her parents. She didn't want another confrontation, and she wasn't ready to explain what was happening—not yet.

That night, as the house fell silent once again, Layla retrieved the box. She selected one of the bottles at random, its label reading clarity.

Unscrewing the cap, she held the bottle to her nose and inhaled deeply. The scent was unlike anything she had ever experienced—sweet yet earthy, light but grounding. It filled her senses, spreading warmth through her chest and limbs.

She dabbed a small amount onto her fingertips and rubbed it onto her temples, as the note had suggested.

At first, nothing happened. She sat on the edge of her bed, waiting, her eyes fixed on the faint glow of the streetlamp outside her window.

And then, a wave of dizziness hit her.

It wasn't unpleasant—more like the sensation of standing too quickly after sitting for too long. Her vision blurred slightly, and the room seemed to tilt ever so gently.

Layla closed her eyes, steadying herself with her hands. The dizziness passed as quickly as it had come, but when she opened her eyes again, the world felt... different.

Chapter 5: The King

Layla was no longer in her room. Instead, she is in a wide, open space under the afternoon sky. The air feels dry and still. There's a faint smell of dust and plants in the breeze. The ground beneath her feet feels hard and cracked.

Layla looks around, trying to figure out where she is. She notices a few hills here and there. Everything feels quiet here. To Layla's left, there's a river glinting in the sunlight. The only sound around here is of the water.

Far ahead, something catches her eye. At first, it looks like a blur in the distance. But as Layla steps closer, she realises it's not something natural. It's too straight, too sharp. Perhaps it's a wall – or a building.

Before she could step any closer, two men emerged from behind the bushes. They are wearing an armour and carrying a spade. "Hold there, young lady. State your name and purpose."

Layla stood frozen. She had barely registered the men's words before the sound of hooves and wheels on the dry ground erupted through the silence. Turning her head quickly, her eyes widened in shock as a grand carriage came into view, pulled by two strong horses. The carriage was enormous. It had golden embellishments along the edges, and they shone brightly in the sun.

When the carriage came to a halt, Layla could see the figure inside. A tall, regal man sat there, dressed in rich robes of crimson and gold. His face was framed by a crown of intricate silver work. His presence was powerful, commanding attention without him needing to say a word. This was no ordinary man. Layla quickly recognised him from her history textbook. This was the King of Babylon.

The men with the spades stepped back and bowed low as the king dismounted the carriage. His boots hit the ground softly. The air seemed to grow thicker, the world around Layla quieter, as if all of nature was holding its breath.

The king's sharp eyes landed on Layla, and for a moment, she felt like a book being read from cover to cover. His gaze wasn't angry, but there was an unsettling weight to it—like he knew every little thought tumbling around in her head, including the one where she'd convinced herself she'd marry a prince.

His lips twitched, almost as if he wanted to smile but thought better of it. Instead, his expression settled into something halfway between pity and amusement. When he finally spoke, his voice was smooth, calm, and just a little too knowing. It wasn't cruel, exactly, but it wasn't comforting either. If voices could pat someone on the head while shaking their own, his just did.

"Who are you, child? And why are you wandering so far from the safety of the city walls?"

Layla froze like a startled cat. Her mind scrambled for a response, but her tongue seemed to have decided it wasn't getting involved. She stared at the imposing King of Babylon, whose piercing eyes softened slightly, probably mistaking her stunned silence for fear.

"I..." she began, but the words got stuck somewhere between her throat and the scorching air.

The king raised an eyebrow, his gaze narrowing ever so slightly as if trying to read a book she hadn't given him permission to open. "Ah, so you're one of *those*—the quiet ones. I see." He stepped closer, his voice calm but carrying a weight that made her knees wobble. "There is no need to be frightened. You are far from home, aren't you? But rest assured, you're safe here... for now."

Layla hesitated, unsure whether to trust him, but before she could come up with a clever response (or any response, really), the king tilted his head and gave her a knowing look. It was as if he *knew* about Layla's darkest thoughts—the one that's been disturbing her for what feels like forever. The one where she believed she might get married to a prince. Did he? No, surely not. She told herself it was impossible, but his expression said otherwise.

"Come," he said with a faint sigh, as though pitying her. "You may follow me to the city. There's something about you, girl—something... peculiar."

Layla blinked. What was that supposed to mean? Did he know? No, he couldn't. Could he? Her mind raced as she fell into step behind him, her sandals kicking up little clouds of dust.

The walk to the city felt endless. Layla's nerves buzzed, and her thoughts kept circling back to the jinn's words: *You will marry a prince.* Every now and then, she stole a glance at the king, wondering if he had a prince in mind. Maybe he was thinking of his son? Maybe it was all part of a sick plan by the royalty to get to meet her.

But her grand visions were interrupted when they reached the city gates. Two guards snapped to attention, their hands resting on their swords. "Your Majesty," they said in unison, bowing deeply.

"Bring *her* inside," the king instructed, glancing at Layla.

The guards exchanged curious looks, but they didn't dare question him. Layla felt their eyes on her as she followed the king into the bustling city. Everyone they passed bowed or murmured respectful greetings. It seemed like the whole world knew who the king was—except for Layla, who still wasn't entirely sure where she was or what was happening.

The city was alive with noise and colour, but Layla's attention was fixed on the towering palace ahead. It was massive. Her heart raced as they approached the entrance.

"Who are you looking for?" she finally dared to ask, her voice small but steady.

The king glanced at her with a faint smirk. "You," he said simply.

Layla blinked. "Me?"

"Yes, you."

Her heart did a flip. This *had* to be about the prophecy. Of course it was! Who else could it be about? *You will marry a prince.* She almost smiled, but then the king added, "Come along. You'll meet the Prince of Babylon soon enough."

Layla barely noticed her surroundings as they entered the palace. Her mind was too busy replaying the words of the prophecy over and over again like a tune.

The king led Layla through the palace with the flair of someone who had clearly rehearsed this walk a thousand times—back straight, robes flowing dramatically, and not a hair out of place. The palace itself was ridiculously magnificent, with columns so tall they looked like they were holding up the sky and artwork so detailed it could probably file a lawsuit for being mistaken as real life. Layla tried to keep up, though her neck was getting sore from constantly craning it to take everything in. Was that a gold statue? Of a cow? Why not?

When they finally entered a massive chamber, Layla was relieved. She wasn't sure if her legs or her brain had been more overwhelmed by the sensory overload. The room smelled like an exotic mix of spices and flowers, with a feast-worthy table in the centre that screamed, *I am rich and important.* A servant appeared out of nowhere, ninja-like, and poured her a drink that looked far too fancy for her dusty hands.

"This is where you'll rest," the king declared with a sweeping gesture, as though he'd personally built the room with his bare hands. "The city will welcome you as one of its own."

Layla nodded, mostly because her jaw was too slack from all the grandeur to form actual words. She couldn't bring herself to say thank you—not because she wasn't grateful but because it felt like "thank you" wasn't big enough for this whole situation. Also, her brain was still screaming, *What's happening?*

The king sat across from her, folding his hands in a way that said *I'm wise and probably about to say something cryptic.* "There is much I could offer you," he began, "but in the royal world, everything comes at a price." Layla wasn't sure if he was warning her or just being dramatic, but either way, she felt like she was in a royal job interview without a résumé.

Before she could respond—or figure out what on earth was happening—the chamber doors swung open. A tall, regal-looking man strolled in, radiating. His dark, curly hair practically glowed, and his finely tailored clothes were enough to make even the walls jealous. Layla immediately knew he was someone important. It was the way he walked, like the floor should be honoured to support his weight.

"This is my son, Prince Ismail," the king announced proudly. "He is the future of Babylon."

Layla's brain, which had been running at half-speed trying to process everything, suddenly short-circuited. *Prince? As in THE prince? Like, prophecy-level prince?* Her heart skipped a beat, though she wasn't sure if it was nerves, excitement, or the very real possibility she was dreaming.

The prince gave her a polite nod, his expression unreadable but far too calm for someone meeting a prophecy-laden stranger. "Greetings," he said, his voice smooth as honey. Layla managed to nod back, though she felt like her face was doing something awkward.

The king, apparently oblivious to the growing awkward tension, grinned like a man with a plan. "I've been thinking," he said, his tone brimming with enthusiasm. "Ismail, you should consider this young for marriage."

Layla nearly choked on her fancy drink. *What?!* Her? For THE Prince of Babylon? She was still trying to figure out how she'd gotten to the palace, let alone wrap her head around being marriage material.

Ismail's reaction, however, was what made her jaw drop. The prince's face twisted in a mixture of shock and discomfort. He cleared his throat, glanced at his father, and said, "Father... I already have a wife."

Layla blinked. *Oh.* Well, that was awkward.

The king's grin faltered, his eyes narrowing like a man whose brilliant plan had just hit a wall. "A wife, yes," he said slowly, as if chewing on the word. "But consider the future of Babylon. There are alliances to form, and—"

"Father," Ismail interrupted, his tone respectful but firm, "no."

Layla, caught in the middle of this royal father-son standoff, suddenly wished she could turn invisible. The air grew so tense it felt like the gilded columns themselves were holding their breath.

Finally, the king sighed, his shoulders slumping slightly. "Very well," he said, sounding more like a disappointed father than a king. He turned to Layla, his tone softening. "This is all a lot to take in, I'm sure. But you are here for a reason. Perhaps it is not what I think, but time will tell."

Layla nodded, unsure of what to say. She felt like a chess piece in a game she didn't know the rules to. As the prince glanced at her one last time before leaving the room, she couldn't help but feel like she had stepped into a story far bigger than herself—one that seemed to involve a lot of misunderstandings, awkward silences, and, apparently, a prophecy.

***

Days turned into weeks, and Layla began to settle into the grand palace of Babylon. The king kept his promise to protect her, but in the bustling halls filled with intrigue, she remained the most baffling enigma of all. Not least because of the way the people referred to her.

"Have you seen her today?" one servant whispered, glancing over their shoulder as they scrubbed the marble floors.

"The stranger?" the other muttered back, lowering their voice. "The woman living in the palace?"

"Yes. Have you heard what people are saying about her?"

"Oh, I've heard plenty." The servant leaned in, eyes gleaming with curiosity. "Some say she's bewitched the King, that he's under some kind of spell."

"Others say she's sick," the first servant added, shaking their head. "That the King only keeps her here out of pity."

"Or maybe she's a runaway noble from some faraway land," another voice chimed in from the shadows.

They all fell silent as footsteps echoed down the corridor. The whispers stopped, but the questions remained. Who was she really? And why had the King allowed her to stay?

The rumor started as a whisper, slipping through the palace halls like a breeze through an open window. A young woman—beautiful, mysterious, a stranger—was living under the King's protection. No one knew where she came from or why she was here, but speculation filled in the gaps.

Eventually, the rumor traveled across the vast deserts and silk-laden trade routes, reaching the extravagant court of Isfahan. It was here that the tale fell upon the ears of a certain prince—one known for his many interests, none of which involved restraint.

"The King of Babylon has a guest," someone said lightly over a lavish feast, pouring wine into a golden cup.

"A guest?" the Prince mused, raising an eyebrow.

"A young woman." A pause. "A striking one."

There was a flicker of amusement in the Prince's dark eyes, a slow, knowing smile curving his lips.

By the time the next day arrived, the news had settled like a quiet promise in the halls of Isfahan. The Prince of Isfahan was making plans. Soon, he would see this woman for himself.

One quiet evening, Layla sat in the palace's courtyard, under the fading light of a deep orange sunset. She wasn't alone for long. From the shadows stepped a figure—handsome, mysterious, and dressed in the finest silks Babylon had to offer.

"Layla," the man said, his voice low and soft.

Layla turned quickly. It wasn't Prince Ismail, the king's son who seemed perpetually distracted by his duties, but someone else entirely.

"Prince Isfahan," he introduced himself with a slight bow. "I'm sorry for startling you. I've been meaning to visit."

"In secret?" Layla asked, arching an eyebrow. "Why all the sneaking about?"

The prince hesitated, glancing over his shoulder like a thief caught red-handed. "Because my father forbids it. He doesn't think I should… associate with you or any woman for that matter."

"Why?"

"Well," Prince Isfahan said, rubbing the back of his neck, "he's set on alliances and politics. He'd rather I focus on securing the future of our kingdom. But…" His words trailed off as his gaze met hers. "But I'd rather focus on the present. On you."

Layla's cheeks flushed, though she wasn't entirely sure whether it was from the prince's words or the audacity of him strolling in like this without a second thought.

Their conversation was interrupted by the soft flutter of wings. A bright green parrot swooped down from a nearby tree, perching gracefully on the Prince's shoulder.

Layla's eyes widened. "Oh," she breathed, tilting her head. "I wasn't expecting… company."

The Prince smirked, reaching up to lightly stroke the bird's feathers. "Jealous already?" he teased.

Layla's lips curled into a small smile, her gaze lingering on him. "Should I be?"

He chuckled. "That depends. She has quite the reputation, you know."

Layla leaned in slightly, her voice softer now. "And what about you, Your Highness? Do you have a reputation?"

The Prince studied her for a moment, amusement flickering in his dark eyes. "If I do, I wonder what you've heard."

Layla laughed, shaking her head. "Does it matter? I already know how this ends."

He raised an eyebrow. "Do you?"

The parrot squawked, interrupting them, and the Prince sighed dramatically. "Ah, she keeps me humble."

Layla's gaze flickered to the bird before settling back on him, a playful glint in her eyes. "I think I prefer her quiet."

The Prince leaned in slightly, just enough to make her pulse quicken. "And me?"

Layla's smile deepened. "We'll see."

As the sky darkened and the stars began to peek through the heavens, the prince sighed. "I must go now before someone notices I'm missing."

Layla crossed her arms, half-joking but also half-serious. "If your father catches you, don't blame me."

The prince gave her a charming smile. "Don't worry, I'll be fine. But…" He hesitated, looking almost shy for the first time. "I'll come back. Even if it's in secret."

After the Prince of Isfahan left, Layla sat under the stars, realizing that the chaos of Babylon wasn't something she had stepped into—it was something she had become part of.

The night was warm, the air thick with the scent of blooming jasmine. A soft breeze played with her hair as she tilted her head back, letting the sky swallow her whole.

And then, she saw it.

The moon.

For so many nights, it had been her only companion, a silent witness to her loneliness. She had watched it cry, its light blurred with sadness, as if mourning alongside her. But tonight... tonight was different.

The moon wasn't sad anymore.

It was smiling.

Soft, steady, and full, its glow stretched across the sky like quiet reassurance. As if to say—this is exactly where you are meant to be.

Layla let out a breath she didn't know she was holding. Maybe, for the first time in a long time, she believed it.

Chapter 6: The Suitors

The next morning, Layla woke up to the sound of loud voices outside her window. They weren't just the usual chatter of villagers going about their day. These voices were sharper, firmer, and impossible to ignore. Still half-asleep, she couldn't quite make out what they were saying, but the tone was enough to jolt her awake.

Rubbing her eyes, she got out of bed and shuffled to the window. As she got closer, the words became clearer. The men were speaking urgently, their voices rising and falling, like they were arguing or making some kind of plan. Layla frowned, trying to make sense of their conversation.

Then she heard it. Her name. *Layla.* One of them said it, then another, and then again, as if she were the centre of whatever they were discussing. Her stomach tightened. They were talking about her.

She stared out the window, unsure whether to feel alarmed or curious. For a moment, she just stood there, her mind racing. Finally, she thought, *If they're talking about me, then I should probably be out there, shouldn't I?*

With that, she turned away from the window, her curiosity stronger than her hesitation. Whatever this was about, she knew she couldn't just stay in her room and wonder.

As Layla stepped outside, the chatter stopped abruptly. The men turned to look at her. There was something about their gazes.

They were filled with awe. But why? Standing in the courtyard were three figures, unlike anyone she had ever seen.

The first man stood tall in a deep crimson robe embroidered with gold, the kind that announced he was either very important or very full of himself. His sharp features and piercing gaze made it clear he took himself—and whatever he was up to—very seriously. A curved sword hung at his side, its jewelled hilt catching the sunlight like it had something to prove.

The second man, draped in a cloak of midnight blue, had the kind of smile that made you instantly like him—even if you weren't sure why. His dark eyes carried a quiet, thoughtful intensity, as if he was always sizing up the world but too polite to let on. His hands, calloused yet steady, rested on a staff covered in intricate carvings that seemed just mysterious enough to make you wonder if he knew something you didn't.

The third man, standing slightly apart, was easily the most handsome of the three—not that he seemed to care. His tunic was plain, his boots well-worn, and his hair looked like he had more important things to do than bother with a comb. But there was something about him—a restless energy, a quiet confidence—that made him impossible to ignore.

Layla's heart raced as the realisation dawned on her. These weren't ordinary men. They were princes—strangers from lands far beyond the horizon. And they were here for her for some reason. Could it have something to do with the prophecy?

One of the men of King Babylon who had been speaking earlier stepped forward, his voice steady but charged with importance. "Lady Layla, these three noblemen have travelled great distances, each with the same wish—to win your hand in marriage."

Layla blinked. Then she blinked again. Surely, she had misheard.

"They want what?" she asked, barely suppressing a laugh.

The man who had been speaking earlier—a dignified, overly serious fellow—cleared his throat and repeated, "They wish to marry you."

Layla stared at them, waiting for the punchline. A long pause stretched between them, filled only with the awkward shifting of feet and the occasional rustle of fabric.

Oh. They were serious.

She let out a snort of disbelief. "Right. Because there's nothing more romantic than three complete strangers showing up and announcing, 'Congratulations, we've decided one of us will be your husband!'"

The first prince, a handsome but stiff-looking man, frowned. "It's a great honor."

"Oh, of course," Layla said, nodding sagely. "And I suppose I should just swoon on command? Maybe faint dramatically into the arms of whoever wins?" She placed a hand on her forehead and staggered back for effect.

The second prince sighed. "We mean no offense. This is merely how these things are done."

Layla narrowed her eyes. "You travelled all this way to marry me... and you're just going to draw lots to decide who gets the prize? You don't even want to pretend to be interested?" She gasped, placing a hand over her heart. "What if I have a terrible personality? What if I snore?"

The third prince, the youngest and most restless-looking of the bunch, crossed his arms. "Then it's a gamble we're willing to take."

Layla's eyes twinkled with mischief. Oh, this was too good. If they wanted to play games, then she would make sure they regretted it.

She straightened, clasping her hands behind her back. "Very well," she said. "I accept."

The three princes exchanged glances, surprised by her sudden change in demeanour.

"But," she continued, holding up a finger, "I have three conditions. All of them must be met, or I won't consider a single one of you."

The first prince nodded, his expression serious. "Name them."

Layla smiled sweetly. "First, I will not simply be a wife. I will own land. Not a dowry, not a gift—mine, with full control to do as I please.".

The second prince blinked. "Land?"

"Yes." Layla confidently replied.

The first prince hesitated, then nodded. "That can be arranged."

Layla grinned. They were actually going along with it? Oh, this was going to be fun.

"Second," she said, ""I will take over the throne. Whether as a queen consort or a ruler in my own right, I will not be a figurehead. If you expect me to stand beside you, I demand the same power and authority."

This time, the second prince did a double take. "You want... the throne?"

"Yes," Layla said seriously. "I want to have just as much authority as you do."

The third prince, who had been silent up until now, suddenly grinned. "I like it."

The first prince sighed, rubbing his temples. "Fine. If it means you'll accept, we'll find a way to ."

Layla clapped her hands together. "Wonderful! Now, my final condition—" She paused dramatically. "No pets."

The first prince raised an eyebrow. "No pets?"

"No pets," she repeated. "No dogs, no cats, no exotic beasts. I don't want to wake up with a tiger in my bedroom because one of you has a dramatic flair for collecting dangerous animals."

The second prince frowned. "But I have a falcon."

Layla shrugged. "Then it's me or the falcon."

The first prince's lips pressed into a thin line. "I have hunting hounds."

"Again, me or the hounds."

The third prince groaned. "I have a pet lizard named Gerald. He's very well-behaved."

"I don't care if he writes poetry in his spare time," Layla said. "No pets."

The three princes exchanged looks. This, it seemed, was the real deal-breaker.

After a long silence, the first prince cleared his throat. "Perhaps... we could compromise?"

Layla smiled, leaning in slightly. "Oh, so you'll take away my throne?"

The second prince groaned. "No, just—surely you don't mean no animals at all?"

"I do," Layla said firmly.

The third prince rubbed the back of his neck. "Even Gerald?"

"Yes, even Gerald."

The three men stood there, clearly rethinking their life choices.

The first prince let out a slow breath. "I think... we should discuss this."

Layla beamed. "Of course! Take all the time you need."

The three princes huddled together, whispering furiously. Layla could hear snippets of their conversation.

"...all other conditions make sense, but no pets?"

"...how attached are you to the falcon?"

"...but Gerald has been with me since childhood!"

After what felt like ages, they turned back to her, looking grim.

The first prince squared his shoulders. "We accept your first two conditions."

Layla grinned.

"But," he added, "the no-pets rule is... unacceptable."

Layla gasped in mock horror. "So you're telling me—after all this—you would choose your precious animals over me?"

The second prince looked mildly guilty. The third prince, however, simply shrugged. "Gerald and I have been through a lot."

Layla fought the urge to laugh. "Well, gentlemen, it seems we have reached an impasse."

The three princes looked at each other, then back at her. Slowly, one by one, they stepped back.

"We appreciate your time," the first prince said, bowing. "But we cannot accept."

The second prince gave a polite nod before turning away.

The third prince sighed. "Gerald will be devastated," he said, before following the others.

Layla watched them go, biting the inside of her cheek. She could hear the murmurs of the onlookers, who were clearly baffled by what had just transpired.

As soon as the princes were out of sight, Layla let out a small, victorious sigh and stretched her arms over her head. She felt proud of herself for being able to understand their mockery. Surely, they weren't here to actually marry her. How was it even possible? They must have caught wind of a strange girl believing she's going to marry a prince. The prophecy was nothing but a joke. It has to be.

"Well," she muttered to herself, "that was fun."

And with that, she turned on her heel and strolled back inside, already wondering what sort of nonsense she could stir up next.

Chapter 7: The Drunk

Layla's faith in the prophecy, the one she had clung to for so long, was starting to slip through her fingers. For years, it had been her guiding light, a promise that her life was destined for something special. But now, after the princes had so easily turned her away, it felt like nothing more than an empty tale.

The rejection left her restless. At first, she questioned herself. *Had she asked for too much? Was she being unreasonable? Was the prophecy ever real?* The self-doubt gnawed at her, but it didn't stop there. Before long, her doubts turned into anger.

"What am I even doing here?" she muttered under her breath, pacing the floor of her chambers for what felt like the hundredth time. The palace now felt hollow. Every glittering chandelier and polished marble floor seemed to mock her. She had come here because she believed she was destined to marry a prince, yet none of them had wanted her.

The questions kept piling up in her mind. *Was this her fault, or was the prophecy just a lie?* She didn't know what to believe anymore.

Day after day, her frustration grew. She couldn't shake the feeling that she was stuck in a place where she didn't belong, waiting for something that wasn't going to happen.

One morning, after another sleepless night, Layla had had enough. She needed to get out, to escape the suffocating walls of the palace and the weight of her own thoughts.

She grabbed her shawl and threw it around her shoulders, not caring that it was slightly wrinkled. "I need to clear my head," she muttered to herself.

The palace guards gave her curious glances as she walked past them, but no one stopped her. They probably assumed she was just taking her usual stroll in the courtyard. This time, though, she didn't stop at the gardens. She pushed open the gates and stepped out onto the path leading away from the palace.

The air outside was cool and refreshing. Layla didn't know where she was going, but she didn't care. She just needed to walk, to let her feet carry her somewhere—anywhere—that wasn't the palace.

The path she followed was lined with trees. She wandered aimlessly until she found herself at the edge of a meadow. Here, away from the judgmental eyes and unspoken expectations, Layla finally felt the tension in her chest begin to ease. She took a deep breath and let herself collapse onto a patch of soft grass.

For a while, she sat in silence, letting the world around her blur into a haze of greens and golds. But her thoughts refused to stay quiet. The prophecy kept clinging to her mind.

"What do they expect of me?" she muttered aloud. "To wait forever for a prince who will never come? To change myself to fit their mould?"

Her anger bubbled to the surface again, this time directed not just at the prophecy but at everything and everyone who had ever upheld it.

She picked up a small stone and hurled it into the distance. "What's the point of believing in a destiny that does nothing but disappoint?" she shouted.

Layla sat back, exhausted by her own outburst. The meadow was still now, save for the gentle rustle of the wind. She closed her eyes, letting the quiet wrap around her.

And then, faintly, she heard something—a voice.

It was soft, almost melodic, and it seemed to come from the grove of trees just beyond the meadow. Layla's brow furrowed as she sat up. The voice was singing along to a tune.

Her heart skipped a beat. Was this another trick of her mind, or was someone truly out there?

Driven by equal parts curiosity and frustration, she stood and began to walk toward the sound. Whatever it was, it couldn't possibly make her day worse.

Layla followed the soft, melodic tune. The trees were dense here. The singing grew louder with each step, almost mournful melody that seemed to wrap around her thoughts and draw her closer.

As she pushed through the underbrush, she spotted a figure stumbling through the trees. It was a man dressed in a tattered cloak that looked far too fine for someone wandering the woods. He swayed as he walked, holding a silver flask in one hand and humming along to the tune Layla had heard.

"Hello?" she called out hesitantly.

The man froze mid-step, then turned—or at least, his body did. Layla blinked, her breath catching in her throat. The man had no head.

Her heart pounded in her chest as she tried to make sense of what she was seeing. His movements were erratic. Then, as if in slow motion, he tipped backward and fell with a dull thud onto the ground.

Layla stood frozen for a moment, her mind racing. This must be a trick. A prank. Some cruel joke. But as she stared at the motionless body, she realized there was no one else around, no signs of anyone setting up such an elaborate ruse.

Cautiously, she stepped closer. The man's body was real—solid, breathing, and very much alive despite the glaring absence of his head.

"Are you… are you alright?" she asked, her voice trembling.

A muffled voice responded, startling her. "Over here."

Layla jumped, spinning around to look for the source of the voice. It wasn't coming from the man's body. It was coming from somewhere to her left. She turned and saw nothing but trees.

"Here!" the voice said again, a little more impatiently this time.

She looked down and gasped. Resting against the roots of a tree was the man's head. His dark hair was matted, and his expression was one of mild annoyance as if this sort of thing happened to him all the time.

"Could you help me out?" the head asked, blinking up at her.

Layla gaped, her mind struggling to comprehend the situation. "You—you're talking," she stammered.

The head sighed. "Yes, and I'm also quite separated from my body at the moment. A little assistance would be appreciated."

Shaking herself out of her stupor, Layla knelt down and picked up the head as carefully as if it were made of glass. "What happened to you?" she asked.

The head smirked. "Long story. Let's just say wine and spells don't mix well."

She carried the head back to the body, her hands trembling slightly. Setting it down on the grass, she rummaged through her shawl, pulling out a strip of fabric she had tucked away for emergencies.

"I… I'll try to bandage you up," she said, though she wasn't sure how one went about treating a severed head.

The head chuckled. "It's not quite as bad as it looks. Just hold it in place, and I'll do the rest."

Layla hesitated but followed his instructions, pressing the head against the neck of the body. As soon as she did, a strange warmth spread through her hands, and she felt a faint hum, like the vibration of an unseen energy.

Before her eyes, the head fused back onto the body. The man groaned softly and rolled his shoulders as if testing them out. "Ah, much better," he said, tilting his neck from side to side.

Layla stumbled back, staring at him in shock. "Who—what—are you?"

The man dusted off his tattered cloak, wincing slightly as he stretched his arms. He offered Layla a crooked smile, his hazel eyes glinting with mischief. "What am I?" he echoed her question. "Well, I could tell you I'm a prince, but judging by your expression, you might not believe me."

Layla frowned, her shock giving way to irritation. "A prince? You expect me to believe that? Princes don't usually lose their heads—literally!"

He chuckled, his laughter warm but tinged with embarrassment. "Fair enough. Let's just say I'm not exactly a typical prince. My name's Samir. And you are?"

"Layla," she replied cautiously, her curiosity getting the better of her. "And what exactly were you doing out here? You were—" she gestured at the ground where his head had been moments earlier, "—in pieces."

Samir shrugged as if it were nothing more than a minor inconvenience. "A mix of bad decisions and worse wine. Let's just say magic doesn't pair well with either."

Layla opened her mouth to demand a clearer explanation, but before she could speak, a commanding voice echoed through the grove.

"Samir!"

The sound was sharp and authoritative, and it sent a shiver down Layla's spine. Both she and Samir turned to see a tall, imposing figure emerge from the trees. The man was dressed in elaborate robes of gold and crimson. His dark eyes narrowed as they landed on Layla.

"What is the meaning of this?" the man demanded, his gaze darting between Samir and Layla.

Samir's playful demeanour vanished, replaced by a sheepish grin. "Ah, Father! Fancy meeting you here. I was just—uh—stretching my legs."

The man did not look amused. His voice was cold and clipped. "Stretching your legs? In such a state? And who is this woman? Did I not tell you to stay away from women unless I allow you to court her?" He turned his piercing gaze on Layla, and she felt as though he could see right through her.

"I'm nobody," Layla blurted, taking an instinctive step back. "I mean, I just found him like this. I was trying to help—"

"Help?" the man interrupted. "And how exactly does a stranger happen upon my son in such a peculiar situation?"

Samir held up his hands in a placating gesture. "Now, Father, let's not jump to conclusions. Layla here is innocent. I owe her my thanks, actually. She was kind enough to lend me a hand—literally."

The man's brow furrowed, and his gaze hardened. "Do not mock me, boy. This is not the first time your recklessness has brought shame upon our family. You speak of gratitude, but I see nothing here but foolishness."

Samir's smile faltered, and for a moment, he looked like a chastened child. "It wasn't her fault," he said quietly. "I was the one who made the mistake."

Layla watched the exchange, her heart pounding. She had no idea what kind of politics or history was at play here, but she could sense the tension between father and son.

The man turned his attention back to her, his expression unreadable. "You say you were helping my son. Why? What do you hope to gain from this?"

Layla straightened her back, determined not to let fear show. "I wasn't trying to gain anything. I heard someone singing, and when I found him—like that—I couldn't just leave him there."

The man studied her for a long moment, his eyes narrowing slightly. Then, to her surprise, he gave a small nod. "Very well. If what you say is true, then I owe you a debt of gratitude. But know this: my son's carelessness is his burden to bear. Do not involve yourself further in matters that do not concern you."

"Understood," Layla said quickly, eager to avoid any further accusations.

The man turned back to Samir. "You will return to the palace at once. We will discuss this further in private."

Palace. Layla's breath hitched. So, Samir wasn't lying. He was actually a prince. But a prince of where?

Samir groaned but didn't argue. "Yes, Father."

As the king, Samir's father, began to walk away, Samir glanced over his shoulder at Layla, offering her a faint smile. "Thanks again, Layla."

She didn't respond, too stunned to say anything. She watched as the two men disappeared into the trees.

Who exactly was this prince with his strange magic and disapproving father? And why did she feel as though she had seen him somewhere before?

Little did she know, the drunken man she had stumbled upon in the woods wasn't just any prince. He was the Prince of Isfahan, and his escapade had been no accident. It was a test, a way to judge the character of those who sought his hand. And Layla, despite her doubts and frustrations, had just proven herself in ways she couldn't yet understand.

Taking a deep breath, Layla turned back toward the palace. She hadn't found the answers she was seeking, but she had stumbled upon something unexpected—a crack in the veneer of her despair, a thread of intrigue that might just lead her to a new path.

Just then, Layla heard another voice, and it stopped her cold.

At first, it was just a laugh, light and amused, like someone enjoying a private joke. But then came the words, clear and laced with amusement. "One prank, and they get in trouble. It's the same for everyone—humans, jinns, animals. He won't be allowed to leave his palace for long after this."

Layla's stomach dropped. That voice. She knew it too well. How could she not? It had haunted her nights, filled her dreams with unease, and turned her days into a whirlwind of confusion and worry.

It was the voice that had made a prophecy she could never forget: *You will marry a prince.*

Her chest tightened, and she glanced around the dim, empty space, searching for the speaker. But the shadows were thick, hiding what—or who—was there.

And then it came again, softer this time, almost playful. "Still so curious, Layla? Some things never change."

Chapter 8: The Trick

Layla shut herself inside her chamber the moment she returned to the palace, bolting the door behind her as if that could keep the voice out. That voice. The one that had followed her like a shadow.

She paced back and forth, her mind a whirlwind of questions. Whose voice was that? What did it mean?

Her fingers trembled slightly as she pulled off her headpiece and tossed it onto the nearby table. She sank into the cushioned chair by the window, staring out at the endless cityscape of Babylon.

Was the prophecy a lie all along?

A small, bitter laugh escaped her lips. She wouldn't be surprised. A part of her had *always* known it sounded too good to be true. A prince, a grand destiny, a future woven by fate itself—it all seemed like the kind of story an old woman would tell by the fire on a cold night.

And yet, another part of her—perhaps the foolish, stubborn part—had *wanted* to believe it. She had *needed* to believe it. Because if the prophecy wasn't real, then what was she doing here? What was the point of everything she had endured, every choice she had made, every moment she had spent waiting for something that was never meant to happen?

Her hands clenched into fists. *Was she just insane? Had she imagined it all?*

She had been brought to the King of Babylon's palace with the promise of fate guiding her path. But where was her prince? Where was the grand love story she had been promised?

The only man who seemed even *remotely* interested in her was the prince of Isfahan, and even he was hardly the picture of a fairytale suitor. He came and went as he pleased, visiting her every now and then with polite words and carefully measured smiles. But what was the point?

Even if, by some miracle, he *did* wish to marry her, he would need his father's blessing. And the King of Isfahan was not exactly known for his *open-mindedness.*

Layla let out a frustrated sigh and slumped back in her chair. Maybe she had been a fool all along. Maybe she had spent too much time chasing a dream that had never been real to begin with.

And maybe... just maybe... she had been waiting for something that was never meant to come.

Just then, Layla heard a knock at the door. She instantly froze as she knew who it was. The knock was around the same time when the Prince of Isfahan would visit her in secret. For a moment, she thought about pretending she wasn't inside. Maybe if she stayed quiet long enough, he'd just *go away.* But the prince of Isfahan wasn't the type to give up easily.

"Lady Layla," his smooth voice called from the other side. "I know you're in there. Unless, of course, you've suddenly learned the art of invisibility?"

Layla rolled her eyes. Even in her worst moods, he somehow managed to be amusing. *Infuriatingly* amusing.

With a sigh, she pulled herself up and opened the door. There he stood, leaning casually against the doorway, dressed in fine silks with a confident smirk on his lips. His dark eyes studied her face carefully, and for the first time, Layla felt a little exposed—like he could *see through* her, past the forced politeness, past the irritation, straight into the storm inside her head.

"You look like you just lost a duel," he said, stepping inside without waiting for an invitation.

"I didn't," Layla replied flatly. "But I might challenge someone soon if they keep testing my patience."

The prince chuckled and took a seat, stretching his legs out as if this were *his* room instead of hers. "I take it that's a warning for me?"

Layla sighed and sat across from him. She had been so ready to brush him off, but now that he was here, something about his presence made her want to talk. And before she knew it, the words came tumbling out.

"I heard a prophecy when I was a child," she began, staring at the flickering candle on the table. "It said I would marry a prince.

I've spent my whole life chasing that prophecy, thinking it was my fate. I thought that's why I ended up here, in the palace of the King of Babylon. But now…" She hesitated, then took a deep breath. "Earlier today, when I was in the woods, I helped a drunk man. He was lost, completely out of his senses. After I helped him get back on his feet, he left… and then I heard a voice. The same voice from my childhood. It mocked me, saying, 'Some things never change.'"

She looked up, expecting the prince to be at least *somewhat* serious about this. Instead, he laughed. A full, hearty laugh, as if she had just told him the funniest joke in the world.

Layla frowned. "Did I say something amusing?"

"Oh, forgive me," he said, still grinning. "It's just… you poor thing! You've been tormenting yourself over a prank from the *King Jinn?*"

Layla blinked. "The *what?*"

"The King Jinn. He's the Behemoth of Alcoholia," the prince explained, as if it were common knowledge. "Trickster of the unseen world, loves to mess with people for his own amusement. He probably heard you're still suffering because of that childhood prophecy and decided it would be *hilarious* to whisper the same nonsense in your ear again today."

Layla stared at him, utterly speechless. "So you're saying," she began slowly, "that my *entire life's purpose*—the prophecy I've shaped my fate around—was just *a joke?*"

"Not necessarily a *joke*," he said, tapping his chin thoughtfully. "More like… an *experiment?* Maybe the Behemoth of Alcoholia wanted to see how far you'd go for a vague promise. And, well… you *have* gone quite far, haven't you?"

Layla's mouth opened, then closed. She had no words. None. She was too busy trying to decide whether she should scream, cry, or throw something at him.

The prince, however, seemed completely unbothered. He leaned back in his chair, watching her with that same amused glint in his eyes. "Look on the bright side," he said. "At least you know now! No more waiting for a mysterious prince to appear out of nowhere."

Layla folded her arms. "And what if I *still* believe in the prophecy?"

He shrugged. "Then I suppose you'll have to start considering your options." His smirk widened. "You *do* know I'm a prince, don't you?"

Layla groaned and buried her face in her hands. This was *not* how she expected this conversation to go.

Layla peeked at the prince through her fingers, hoping—*praying*—that he would show *some* sign of guilt, or at least a little bit of concern. But no. There he was, lounging in *her* chair like he owned the place, looking as if they were discussing the weather instead of the fact that her entire *life* might have been a trick played by some supernatural prankster.

She sat up straight. "So that's it?" she demanded. "You hear my life's biggest dilemma, the thing that's haunted me since childhood, and your response is—what? A shrug?"

The prince raised an eyebrow. "Would you prefer I gasped dramatically? Clutched my chest in horror? Declared that we must consult the palace mystic at once?" He placed a hand over his heart in mock sincerity. "Oh, dearest Layla, how shall we ever recover from this tragic revelation?"

Layla narrowed her eyes. She was dangerously close to throwing the nearest pillow at his face.

"Unbelievable," she muttered under her breath.

"I'm just saying," the prince continued, completely unbothered, "life is full of surprises. Maybe instead of chasing an old prophecy, you should focus on what's *right in front of you.*"

Layla crossed her arms. "And what exactly is *in front* of me?"

The prince flashed a charming grin and spread his arms. "Me."

Layla groaned. Loudly. "Get out."

The prince laughed as he stood up. "Alright, alright. I'll leave you to *ponder* this new truth." He strolled towards the door, moving with that same easy confidence, as if her entire crisis was nothing more than a passing inconvenience to him. Just before stepping out, he turned back and gave her one last playful smirk.

"Sleep well, Lady Layla. Don't let the Behemoth of Alcoholia whisper in your ear again."

Then, he was gone.

Layla sat there in silence, staring at the door. The audacity. The nerve. The *complete lack of concern!*

She took a deep breath, trying to calm herself, but her mind was already racing. She replayed every conversation, every encounter she had ever had with the Prince of Isfahan. And suddenly, everything made sense.

The prince was *too* relaxed. Too casual. He never spoke about the future. Never mentioned anything *serious* between them. And then there were the *birds*.

She had always thought it was charming, the way he kept all those exotic birds in his private garden. Peacocks, doves, songbirds of every kind. But now she realized—they weren't *just* birds. They were a *metaphor*.

She wasn't the only one he entertained.

Layla clenched her fists. Of course. *Of course!* The prince of Isfahan was exactly what she should have expected—a man born into indulgence, someone who had never known what it was like to *want* for anything. Women surrounded him like his birds, each one admiring him, waiting for his attention, hoping to be the one he favored most.

And she—*she*—had been foolish enough to think he was serious about *her?*

She stood up so fast her chair nearly toppled over.

No. She refused to be just another name in the prince's collection. She had wasted *enough* of her life believing in a prophecy that was probably nothing more than a cosmic joke. But if there was *one* thing she could do now, it was expose this entire mess for what it was.

Tomorrow, the Prince of Jerusalem was arriving in Babylon. He was serious, honorable, and well-respected among all the royal courts. If *anyone* would take her seriously, it was him.

Layla smirked.

The Prince of Isfahan thought this was just a game? That she was just another woman to be charmed and forgotten?

Well, he was about to learn otherwise.

***

The next morning, Layla woke up with a fire in her heart and a plan in her mind. She was *done* playing the fool. Today, she was marching straight into the royal court to expose the Prince of Isfahan for what he truly was—a man who collected women like trinkets and treated them no better than his pet birds.

Dressed in her finest silk gown, she walked into the grand courtroom with her head held high. The hall was buzzing with noblemen, scholars, and visiting royals, all engaged in their usual discussions about politics, war, and—of course—who was secretly seeing whom behind closed doors.

Layla ignored the side glances and whispers as she moved with purpose, her eyes set on the one man she needed to speak to.

The Prince of Jerusalem.

He was a man of wisdom, fairness, and most importantly—he had *zero* tolerance for nonsense. If there was anyone who could bring justice to this ridiculous situation, it was him.

She approached his seat, bowed gracefully, and in a voice loud enough for *everyone* to hear, she said,

"Your Highness, I seek justice."

The room went silent.

The Prince of Jerusalem raised an eyebrow. "Justice, Lady Layla? Who has wronged you?"

Layla crossed her arms. "The Prince of Isfahan."

A *collective gasp* echoed through the court. Conversations stopped. Even the royal scribes put down their quills to listen.

The Prince of Jerusalem leaned forward, intrigued. "And what has the Prince of Isfahan done to earn your wrath?"

Layla lifted her chin. "He has led me to believe there was something real between us, but all the while, he has been entertaining *many* women. He surrounds himself with them as if they are nothing more than his pet birds. He deceives, he charms, and then he forgets." She placed a hand on her hip. "Is this the behavior of a noble prince?"

Murmurs spread through the court. Some nodded in agreement, others exchanged knowing looks.

"Bring in the Prince of Isfahan," the Prince of Jerusalem commanded.

A few minutes later, the doors swung open, and in walked the Prince of Isfahan.

And with him, on his shoulder, was his parrot.

Layla rolled her eyes. *Of course,* the bird was here.

The Prince of Isfahan walked in with his usual relaxed confidence, as if he hadn't just been summoned like a misbehaving child. "To what do I owe this dramatic summons?" he asked, flashing a charming smile.

The Prince of Jerusalem wasted no time. "Lady Layla has made a claim against you. She says you have misled her and that your affections are not as they seem."

The Prince of Isfahan chuckled. "Misled her? I don't recall making any promises."

Before Layla could snap back, the parrot flapped its wings and squawked,

"Too many birds! Too many birds! The prince enjoys *many, many birds!*"

The entire court froze.

The Prince of Isfahan shot the parrot a *look* that could have melted stone. The bird immediately went silent, as if realizing it had just revealed something it shouldn't have.

But it was *too late.*

The other princes in the court turned to one another, clearly amused. Some smirked, others whispered. One even burst out laughing.

The Prince of Jerusalem leaned back in his chair, watching the scene unfold. "Well," he said, tapping his fingers on the armrest, "that was... enlightening."

Layla seized the moment.

"Your Highness, if that wasn't enough proof of his *many distractions,* let me tell you what happened to me last night," she said.

She then explained everything—the mysterious voice, the mocking words, the *exact same voice* she had heard as a child when she was told she would marry a prince.

"It was a trick," she concluded. "A cruel prank by the Behemoth of Alcoholia."

The court erupted into hushed whispers. This was *serious.*

The Behemoth of Alcoholia was no ordinary troublemaker. He was an ancient trickster, a powerful supernatural being who had been known to interfere in the affairs of royals. If he had been playing games with Layla's fate, who knew what else he had meddled in?

The rumor spread like wildfire.

By the afternoon, every noble in the city was whispering about the Behemoth of Alcoholia's prank. By the evening, the news had reached the King of Arabia himself.

And by nightfall, a royal council had been called.

The King of Arabia wanted *answers.*

***

The royal council chamber was packed. Kings, princes, noblemen—they were all there, seated in a grand hall decorated with golden chandeliers and heavy velvet drapes. But despite the luxury, the mood in the room was *anything* but pleasant.

The room buzzed with frustration as one royal after another stood up to share their grievances about the Behemoth of Alcoholia.

"He once switched my royal robes with a beggar's rags before a grand feast! I walked in looking like a *street rat* in front of the entire court!" complained the King of Samarkand, his face red with humiliation.

"He made my prized stallion *speak* during a duel!" shouted the Sultan of Khorasan. "Right when I was about to strike, my horse neighed, 'Are you sure about this, my lord?' I lost the duel out of sheer embarrassment!"

The Emir of Damascus shook his head angrily. "He cursed my royal chef to cook *only* spicy food for an entire month. My tongue still hasn't recovered!"

One by one, the royals poured out their frustrations, each story worse than the last.

Layla sat among them, feeling oddly satisfied. Finally, *finally*, someone was taking this seriously.

Then, just as the murmurs of frustration were reaching their peak, the Prince of Arabia—who had been silent until now—stood up.

And he *was furious*.

"ENOUGH!" he bellowed, slamming his fist on the table. The entire room fell silent.

Then, with slow, deliberate movements, he reached under his royal cloak and pulled out—

A *machine gun.*

Yes. A *machine gun.*

The council chamber *gasped.* A few nobles scooted their chairs back, just in case.

The Prince of Arabia held up his weapon, eyes burning with rage. "I have had *enough* of this Jinn's nonsense! I will *not* be made a fool of! I *swear* on my honor—I will not rest until I find him and make him *pay* for his actions!"

The tension in the room skyrocketed. Some princes nodded in agreement. Others looked deeply concerned. The parrot on the Prince of Isfahan's shoulder muttered, "Oh no, oh no, oh no."

And just like that, the news *spread.*

Word traveled fast—faster than a royal messenger on horseback, faster than an arrow shot from a bow.

By the time the council adjourned, the entire kingdom was whispering about it.

By sunset, the tale had reached the deserts, the forests, and the mountains.

And by nightfall?

It had reached *the Behemoth of Alcoholia himself.*

***

The Behemoth of Alcoholia was lounging in his secret hideout—a grand, floating palace hidden in the clouds—when one of his loyal messengers burst in, panting and out of breath.

"My lord!" the messenger gasped. "You—you need to *run!*"

The Behemoth of Alcoholia, who had been enjoying a golden goblet of enchanted wine, raised an eyebrow. "Run? *Me?*" He laughed. "Don't be ridiculous."

The messenger gulped. "The Prince of Arabia has declared *war* on you! He—he pulled out a *machine gun* in the royal council!"

The Behemoth of Alcoholia froze.

"What… did you just say?"

"The Prince of Arabia! He—he is *furious!* He swore he won't rest until he *hunts you down!*"

For the first time in his *very long* life, the Behemoth of Alcoholia *felt fear.*

His goblet slipped from his fingers and crashed to the floor.

He jumped to his feet. "This is *bad!* This is *very bad!*" He turned to his other messengers, now gathered around. "We need to *move!* Get my horses! No—get my *magic carpets!* No—wait—just *run!*"

And so, *the Behemoth of Alcoholia fled.*

He ran through the deserts of Arabia, then hid in the icy mountains of Persia. But word of the Prince of Arabia's rage *followed him everywhere.*

He crossed the seas, hiding in the dense jungles of India, then in the great cities of China. But the news had *already reached* those lands, too.

Wherever he went, people whispered,

"Have you heard? The Prince of Arabia is after the Behemoth of Alcoholia!"

"They say he has a machine gun!"

"They say he won't stop until he finds him!"

Even the birds in the sky seemed to gossip about it.

The Behemoth of Alcoholia tried *everything*—disguises, spells, even *turning invisible.* But the paranoia followed him.

At night, he would *wake up in a cold sweat,* imagining the Prince of Arabia *bursting through the door* with his machine gun.

For the first time in history, the mighty, mischievous, *all-powerful* the Behemoth of Alcoholia was *terrified.*

And so, he kept running—through deserts, through forests, through every corner of the Earth—never daring to stop.

Because *somewhere* out there, the Prince of Arabia was still looking for him.

And he *meant* what he said.

Chapter 9: The Letter

The whole kingdom was in *chaos*.

Ever since the news spread that the Prince of Arabia was hunting down the Behemoth of Alcoholia, it was all *anyone* could talk about.

Markets were buzzing with the latest gossip. People gathered in tea houses, discussing theories like they were royal advisors themselves.

"I heard the Prince of Arabia has already reached the desert!"

"Nonsense! The Behemoth of Alcoholia fled to the mountains!"

"My cousin's wife's brother's friend swears he saw the Behemoth of Alcoholia hiding in a well!"

Even the palace guards—who were supposed to be *on duty*—were too busy whispering about what would happen when the two finally came face to face.

It was as if the entire kingdom had *held its breath*, waiting for the final showdown.

But *Layla*?

Layla was *not* amused.

She sat in her chamber, staring out of the window, tapping her fingers impatiently on the windowsill.

"So *that's* it?" she muttered. "Everyone's forgotten about the Prince of Isfahan?"

She wasn't *done* with him. Not even *close*.

Layla had gone through *all this trouble*—exposing his lies, making a scene in the royal court, and what happened?

Now, instead of talking about *his* betrayal, everyone was too busy worrying about a *Jinn with a death sentence*.

She folded her arms, fuming.

"That Isfahani peacock is probably sitting in his palace *completely relaxed* while I sit here with unfinished business."

She wasn't going to let him *get away that easily*.

Layla thought for a moment. She needed to get everyone's *attention* back on the real problem.

The Prince of Isfahan was a *master of charm*. He had *too many birds* (both the feathery kind and the metaphorical kind). His entire life was about luxury, indulgence, and keeping up appearances.

But what was the *one* thing that could *truly* ruin him?

His *reputation*.

A slow smile crept onto Layla's lips.

"Oh, I know exactly what to do."

The next morning, Layla put on her finest silk gown, arranged her hair perfectly, and walked straight into the royal courtyard—where all the nobles gathered to discuss *serious* matters.

But instead of important political discussions, the topic of the day was still the Prince of Arabia and the Behemoth of Alcoholia.

Layla, however, had other plans.

She walked right up to a group of noblewomen, who were fanning themselves and gossiping as usual. She leaned in, lowering her voice just enough to make them curious.

Layla took a deep breath, placing a hand over her chest as if steadying herself. She knew exactly how to play this moment.

She leaned in closer to the noblewomen, her eyes shimmering with unshed tears. "It's just… so *tragic*."

The women gasped, hanging on to her every word.

"What is, dear Layla?" one of them asked, fanning herself faster.

Layla let out a soft, trembling sigh. "The Prince of Isfahan…" She paused, closing her eyes for a moment. "He broke my heart."

The effect was instant.

The noblewomen gasped. A few palace guards nearby, who had been pretending not to eavesdrop, immediately turned their heads. Even a few noblemen sitting nearby stopped their discussions about the Behemoth of Alcoholia to listen.

"Broke your heart?!" one woman exclaimed, pressing a jeweled hand to her chest. "But—how?"

Layla glanced over her shoulder, making sure the Prince of Isfahan was within earshot. He was standing by the fountain, laughing with some dignitaries, completely unaware that his day was about to take a sharp turn for the worse.

She lowered her voice, making the noblewomen lean in closer. "He led me on for months… whispering sweet words, making me believe I was special to him. And then…" She took a deep, shaky breath. "Then, I discovered the truth."

The women were hooked. "What truth?"

Layla hesitated, as if the words were too painful to say. And then, in a voice just loud enough for the surrounding crowd to hear, she whispered:

"He never intended to marry me. To him, I was just… another bird in his collection."

The courtyard froze.

Several noblemen exchanged glances. A few guards muttered under their breath. And the noblewomen? They looked horrified.

The Prince of Isfahan, finally noticing the shift in atmosphere, turned his head, frowning.

Layla didn't stop there. She placed a hand over her heart, her expression the perfect mixture of heartbreak and quiet strength.

"I was so naive," she continued. "I believed in the prophecy. I believed that fate had brought me to him. But the whole time, he was just… playing a game."

She let out a bitter laugh, shaking her head. "Once, I told him that pomegranates were an elixir of youth. And soon after, he sent me pomegranates, as if he had taken my words to heart, as if he cared." She scoffed softly, eyes darkening. "And then, later, he sent me apples. Apples, which in Greek mythology are signs of courtship. What was I to think? How was I not to believe he meant something by it?"

A murmur spread through the crowd like wildfire.

"That's awful!" one of the noblewomen cried.

"How could he?" another muttered.

"I always thought he was too charming to be serious about any woman," a nobleman said, shaking his head.

By now, the entire courtyard was talking. And the Prince of Isfahan? He stood frozen by the fountain, his usual confident smirk replaced by something dangerously close to panic.

His parrot, perched on his shoulder, picked up on the mood and helpfully squawked, "Too many birds! Too many birds!"

The prince glared at it. "Not. Now."

Layla, still playing the role of the wounded heroine, sighed and turned away slightly, as if she couldn't bear to look at him. "I suppose I should be grateful. At least I know the truth now. At least I can warn other women before they fall for the same tricks."

That did it.

The noblewomen turned on the prince.

"You toyed with Layla?" one of them snapped, her fan snapping shut like a weapon.

"She is a guest, and you broke her heart?!"

A group of noblemen shook their heads in disappointment. "Not very honourable, Isfahani."

Even a palace guard muttered, "Shameful, truly."

The prince's face had gone pale. He *opened* his mouth, then *closed* it. Then opened it again.

"Now, wait just a—"

But before he could defend himself, his parrot *squawked* again, this time much *louder*.

"Too many birds! Too many birds!"

A stunned silence fell over the courtyard.

And then—

Laughter.

First, just a few chuckles. Then full-blown *howls* of laughter from the noblemen, the guards, even some of the dignitaries.

The noblewomen, however, were *not* amused.

"See? Even his own bird *admits it!*" one of them said, furious.

The Prince of Isfahan turned on his parrot. "You *traitor*."

Layla, meanwhile, simply stood there, looking *heartbroken yet dignified*. It was *perfect*.

By now, the damage was done. The Prince of Isfahan's reputation had taken a serious hit. The noblewomen were furious with him. The noblemen were mocking him. And the guards? They were definitely going to tell *everyone* what happened.

Layla bit the inside of her cheek to stop herself from smiling.

Revenge? Oh, it tasted *delicious*.

The prince, realizing he had completely *lost control* of the situation, shot one last glare at Layla before storming off, his parrot flapping after him.

Layla simply watched him go, lifting her cup of pomegranate juice to her lips.

"Now *that's* how you handle a scoundrel," she murmured.

Layla was still basking in the *sweet, sweet* glow of her victory when she heard hurried footsteps behind her.

She turned, and there he was—*again.*

The Prince of Isfahan.

But this time, he wasn't swaggering in like he owned the place. No. His usual smirk was *gone*, replaced by a look of pure, dramatic desperation. His robe was slightly *askew*, his turban looked like it had been *tugged* in frustration, and—most importantly—he was holding something in his hand.

A letter.

The entire courtyard went *silent*.

He strode right up to Layla, eyes locked on hers, and held out the letter with a *flourish.*

"Layla," he said, his voice thick with emotion, "I *never* led you on. I *love* you."

A *gasp* rippled through the crowd.

Layla narrowed her eyes. "Oh?"

The prince nodded solemnly, holding up the letter like it was some ancient relic of love. "This… this is proof."

Layla raised an eyebrow. "What is that?"

The prince *exhaled deeply*, as if he were about to reveal something *profound*. He turned to the noblemen and women who were watching with bated breath.

"This…" he said, voice trembling, "is a letter I wrote to Layla long ago. A letter I *never* had the courage to send."

Layla crossed her arms. "And now you *conveniently* remembered it?"

The prince ignored the sarcasm. He *dramatically* unfolded the letter, revealing *dark red writing* scrawled across the page.

The noblewomen *gasped*.

"*It's written in blood!*" one of them shrieked.

A murmur spread through the court.

"In *blood?!*"

"Truly, his love *knows no bounds!*"

Layla *blinked*.

She leaned forward slightly, staring at the letter. The red writing *was* impressive. It had dried unevenly, creating an almost *tragic* effect. Some of the letters had smudged, as if written in a *moment of deep despair.*

Layla narrowed her eyes.

Something about it felt... *off.*

She turned to the prince. "Whose blood?"

The prince hesitated. "...Mine."

Layla tilted her head. "Are you *sure?*"

The prince's jaw tightened. "Yes."

Layla took a step closer, folding her hands behind her back. "You're saying you took a *knife*, sliced open your own hand, and used your own blood to write this?"

The prince cleared his throat. "Yes. That's exactly what I did."

Layla nodded slowly, her expression unreadable. Then she reached out, took the letter, and *sniffed* it.

The prince *froze.*

The noblemen and women *stared.*

Layla took another sniff. Then, she *grinned.*

"This is *chicken blood.*"

The prince went *rigid*.

The noblewomen *gasped again—*but this time in *horror*.

"*Chicken blood?!*"

Layla turned to face the crowd, waving the letter in the air. "Yes! This fool went to the kitchen, found a dead chicken, squeezed the life out of it, and wrote a love letter!"

The courtyard *erupted*.

"*You used CHICKEN BLOOD?!*"

"*That's not romantic—that's horrifying!*"

"I *kissed* his hand last week!" one noblewoman shrieked, wiping her mouth furiously.

The prince's face turned *red* as his reputation took yet another *plummet*.

Even the palace *guards* were shaking their heads in disappointment. One leaned over to another and muttered, "Man wrote a love letter in *poultry juice*."

Layla turned back to the prince, tapping her chin thoughtfully. "Tell me… when, exactly, did you *selflessly* write this letter?"

The prince hesitated. "I… I don't recall the exact date…"

Layla nodded. "Mmm-hmm. And did you... perhaps... *enjoy a roasted chicken* that same night?"

The prince *winced.*

The noblemen *burst out laughing.*

Layla took a step back, crossed her arms, and sighed dramatically. "I have to say, Prince... I expected *more* from a man of your *reputation.*"

One of the noblewomen huffed. "I feel *betrayed!* I *thought* he was a romantic!"

A nobleman clapped the prince on the back. "Looks like the only true love he had was *for chicken.*"

Another noble laughed. "I bet he whispered sweet nothings to it before he *cooked* it!"

Layla turned to the prince with a *smirk.* "So tell me, Your Highness... do you *actually* love me? Or was this whole thing just another one of your games?"

The prince *looked* at her.

Looked at the *crowd.*

Looked at the *parrot.*

Looked at the *letter written in chicken blood.*

He didn't know what to say. Thankfully, he didn't have to.

The courtyard was still buzzing with laughter and gossip when a sudden *boom* echoed through the palace gates. A wave of silence spread over the nobles. Heads turned. Fans froze mid-air. The laughter died instantly.

And then—*he* appeared.

The King of Isfahan.

Furious.

His robes billowed behind him like a storm cloud. His sharp, lined face was twisted in rage, his piercing eyes scanning the crowd with the weight of a man who *demanded* obedience.

The guards at the entrance stood *frozen*, too afraid to even announce his arrival. He didn't need an introduction. The moment he set foot inside the courtyard, everyone knew—trouble had arrived.

Layla's fingers tightened around the silk of her gown.

Oh, this can't be good.

The king's gaze landed on his son first. The Prince of Isfahan, who had barely made it past the fountain, stopped dead in his tracks. His face went pale.

The parrot, sensing *immediate danger*, wisely took off, disappearing into the palace roof beams.

The king didn't even look at Layla at first. His anger was focused entirely on his son.

"What," he thundered, his voice shaking the very air, "is *this nonsense*?"

The crowd shrank back. Even the palace guards, who had seen their fair share of royal tempers, subtly took a step away.

The prince swallowed. "Father, I—"

"You have *embarrassed* this family," the king snapped, cutting him off. "A love letter written in chicken blood?" He spat the words like they burned his tongue. "Are you a *prince* or a butcher?"

The prince opened his mouth. Then closed it. There was simply *no* good answer to that question.

The noblemen and women held their breath. This was getting *interesting*.

The king's furious gaze *finally* landed on Layla.

She lifted her chin. If he expected her to look away in shame, he was sorely mistaken.

His expression darkened further. "And *you.*"

The courtyard tensed.

Layla's stomach twisted, but she forced herself to remain still.

"I warned you," the king hissed. "I *warned* you not to meddle with my son."

Layla raised an eyebrow. "Did you? I must have missed that royal decree."

A murmur rippled through the crowd. Some noblewomen covered their mouths in shock. Did she just—*talk back* to the King of Isfahan?

The prince closed his eyes briefly, as if praying for divine intervention.

The king took a menacing step forward. "Do you think this is a *game*, girl?" His voice was low, dangerously quiet now. "You have ruined my son's name. You have humiliated my family."

Layla crossed her arms. "Your son did that *all on his own*."

More gasps.

The prince inhaled sharply. His father's expression turned murderous.

The king clenched his fists. "You are a *curse*, Layla. Ever since you walked into my son's life, he has been nothing but a fool."

Layla tilted her head. "I don't control your son. He's perfectly capable of being a fool on his *own*."

A *loud gasp* swept the crowd. Someone *actually* dropped their teacup.

The king's eyes flashed.

Layla had seen men *furious* before. She had seen tempers boil over, seen nobles throw fits. But this? This was different. This was *dangerous*.

The king straightened, his voice ringing across the courtyard. "I have had **enough.**"

A heavy silence fell.

Then—he turned to the palace guards.

"**Seize her.**"

For the first time, Layla's breath *caught*.

The prince's head snapped up. "*What?!*"

The guards hesitated. They had not *expected* this turn of events.

Layla *forced* herself to keep her expression calm, even as her heart pounded in her chest. "You're making a mistake."

The king's lip curled. "No, girl. *You* made the mistake."

The guards took a step forward.

The crowd erupted into whispers.

"He's arresting her?"

"But... why?"

"What crime did she commit?"

Layla stood her ground. "What exactly am I being accused of?"

The king's expression was cold. "Treason."

A *wave* of shock swept the courtyard.

"Treason?!" someone gasped.

"For *what*?" Layla demanded.

The king's voice was sharp as a blade. "For manipulating my son. For *plotting* against the royal house of Isfahan. For bringing shame to the nobility."

Layla *laughed*. It was short, sharp, and full of disbelief. "You mean for *hurting your pride*."

The king's eyes flashed. "For *disrupting* the peace of this kingdom."

The prince *finally* snapped out of his shock. "Father, this is insane!" He rushed forward, grabbing the king's arm. "Layla did *nothing wrong!*"

The king yanked his arm away.

"You defend *her*?" His voice was low, dangerous.

The prince *hesitated.* The entire kingdom was watching.

He swallowed. "She's *innocent.*"

The king's expression twisted in disgust. "You are *weak.*"

The prince *flinched.*

Layla watched it all, her mind racing.

This wasn't just about *her.*

This was about power. The king wasn't punishing her because of some *imaginary crime.* He was making an example out of her. He wanted to *prove* his authority. To remind his son—and everyone else—who truly held control.

Layla's hands clenched at her sides.

She had won against the prince. She had made him look like a fool.

But she had underestimated the *real* enemy.

The king turned to the guards. "Take her to the dungeons."

The crowd *exploded* into whispers.

"She's really being arrested?"

"This isn't fair!"

"She only exposed the prince's lies!"

The guards hesitated.

The prince looked *horrified.* "Father, *don't do this!*"

Layla felt a sharp grip on her arm.

Her heart pounded, but she refused to show fear.

The prince *panicked.* He turned to the crowd. "Do none of you have anything to say?!"

Silence.

Everyone was watching.

But no one moved.

Because no one wanted to be the next *target.*

The prince's hands clenched. His jaw tightened.

Layla could see it—the moment he realized he couldn't stop this.

Not without risking himself.

Not without *challenging* his father.

And he *wasn't brave enough* to do that.

Layla exhaled slowly. Then, she looked the king *dead in the eye*.

"You can throw me in the dungeons," she said calmly. "But you can't erase the truth."

The king *snorted*. "Truth is what I decide it to be."

The guards started to pull her away.

Layla didn't struggle.

She simply turned her head—locking eyes with the prince one last time.

His face was pale. His hands were fists.

But he didn't move.

Layla's lips curled slightly. "Goodbye, Your Highness."

And then, just like that—she was dragged from the courtyard.

The moment she disappeared, the whispers *exploded*.

The Prince of Isfahan stood frozen, his mind screaming.

And in the midst of all the chaos, someone murmured:

"The prince let her take the fall."

And just like that—his reputation took its final, fatal blow.

Chapter 10: The Reckoning

The cold iron shackles dug into Layla's wrists as the guards led her through the dark corridors of the palace. She kept her head high and her face calm, pretending she wasn't afraid. But inside, fear twisted in her stomach like a tight knot.

How had things gone so wrong?

She had only spoken the truth. She had only exposed the Prince of Isfahan for what he really was. But now, instead of him facing any consequences, she was the one being dragged away like a criminal. The King of Isfahan had been furious. He had always disliked her. Now, he had finally found a reason to get rid of her.

The guards stopped in front of a heavy wooden door. One of them pulled out a large iron key, shoved it into the lock, and turned it. The door creaked open, revealing a dark, damp cell. The air smelled of mold and wet stone. A single torch burned weakly on the far wall, giving off just enough light to see the cold floor.

"Inside," one of the guards said, shoving her forward.

Layla stumbled but caught herself before she fell. She wouldn't let them see her weak. She stepped into the cell, and before she could turn around, the door slammed shut behind her. She was alone now.

She let out a slow breath and leaned against the rough wall. She had fought so hard to appear fearless in front of the king, in front of all those watching eyes. But now, with no one around, she could finally admit it. She was scared.

What was going to happen to her?

Would they execute her? Would she be left in this dungeon until she was forgotten? The thought sent a chill down her spine. She pulled her knees up to her chest and wrapped her arms around them.

She never wanted any of this. She never meant to get caught up in royal politics. She was just a lost girl who had somehow found her way to Babylon. She hadn't even known where she was at first. One moment, she was lost in her thoughts, and the next, she was standing in the grandest city she had ever seen.

The King of Babylon had taken her in. He had given her shelter, treated her kindly, and made her feel safe for the first time in a long time. But now, she was sitting in a dungeon in a foreign land, condemned for something she didn't even do.

The King of Isfahan had never trusted her. She knew that from the moment she first met him. He had always looked at her with suspicion, as if waiting for her to make a mistake. And now, in his eyes, she had made the biggest mistake of all—getting too close to his son.

Layla clenched her fists. Was it such a crime to want justice? Was it so wrong to refuse to be treated like a fool?

The worst part was, no one seemed to care that she was being punished unfairly. Everyone was too busy talking about the Prince of Arabia and his hunt for the Behemoth of Alcoholia. No one was thinking about her, sitting here in the dark, waiting for a fate she couldn't control.

And the Prince of Isfahan?

He had done nothing.

Layla had seen the look on his face when she was taken away. He had looked shocked. Maybe even guilty. But he hadn't stopped it. He hadn't spoken up. He had let his father condemn her.

So much for love.

She should have known better. A man like him—who was used to luxury, to admiration, to being surrounded by women—was never going to fight for her.

Layla took a deep breath. She wouldn't cry. She wouldn't let herself fall apart. If no one was going to help her, she would help herself.

She wasn't finished yet. Not by a long shot.

***

The Prince of Isfahan sat in his grand chamber, but for the first time, it didn't feel grand at all. The soft silk cushions, the golden lamps, the carved wooden furniture—it all felt empty. He was supposed to be a prince, living in luxury, but right now, all he felt was guilt.

Layla was in a dungeon because of him.

He leaned forward, his elbows resting on his knees, his fingers tangled in his thick, dark hair. He had spent the whole evening replaying everything in his head, but no matter how many times he thought about it, the conclusion was the same. He had failed her.

And the worst part?

She thought he was just some womanizer.

A small, bitter laugh escaped his lips. A womanizer. He had been called many things in his life—charming, reckless, arrogant—but never had a word stung him as much as this one did. If someone had accused him of it before he met Layla, he wouldn't have denied it. In fact, he might have even smirked and accepted it like a badge of honor.

But now?

Now, it felt like a cruel joke.

Because the truth was, ever since he met Layla, she was the only thing on his mind. She had taken over his thoughts, invaded his dreams, and stolen every moment of his peace. No other woman had ever done that to him. No one had ever made him feel this way.

He let out a deep sigh and leaned back, staring at the ceiling. His mind drifted back to that night—the night that changed everything.

It had all started with magic.

He had been so desperate to see her that he had done something foolish. He had played around with potions, hoping to find one that would transport him straight to the Palace of Babylon's garden, where Layla liked to wander at night. He had thought it would be simple. A sip of a potion, a swirl of magic, and—poof—he'd be standing right in front of her, ready to impress her with some poetic nonsense.

But, of course, things hadn't gone as planned.

Instead of teleporting to the garden like a graceful prince, he had ended up losing his head. Literally.

One moment, he was holding the potion bottle in his hand, and the next—his head was rolling across the floor.

He had no idea how it happened. One wrong ingredient? A mispronounced spell? A particularly bad day for magic? He didn't know. All he knew was that he had no head, no idea what to do, and an increasing sense of panic.

So, like any reasonable man in an unreasonable situation, he had picked up his own head and started walking.

At first, it was horrifying. People screamed. A merchant fainted. A dog barked at him like he was a piece of flying meat.

But after some time, he got used to it. He figured he just needed to find a sorcerer, someone who could put his head back where it belonged. He wandered through the streets, trying not to draw attention—although that was difficult when you were carrying your own head under your arm.

And then, somehow, fate brought him to her.

It was a quiet night and a lonely walk in the woods when he saw her. Layla.

She was sitting on a stone bench, looking at the stars, completely unaware that she was about to meet a headless man. He had hesitated for a moment, wondering if he should just turn around and go hide in a cave forever. But something pulled him forward.

So, with all the grace of a man who had lost control of his own body, he stepped out of the shadows. But he didn't want to reveal who he truly was. Something inside urged him to test how Layla would react. So, he pretended to be a drunk man.

She gasped when she saw him, her eyes going wide in shock. For a moment, she just stared at him, probably trying to decide whether to scream or run. But then, something incredible happened.

She didn't run. She didn't scream. She didn't faint like the merchant in the market.

Instead, she rushed toward him.

Before he could process it, Layla was already gently taking his head from his hands. She examined it carefully, as if checking for wounds, her fingers soft against his skin.

Then, with the care of a healer, she guided him to sit down. She pulled out a scarf from her dress—one made of the softest fabric—and wrapped it around his neck. She worked quickly, delicately, as if she had done this a hundred times before.

"There," she said when she was done, stepping back to look at him.

The Prince blinked. His head was still not fully attached, but it was steady now, thanks to her careful bandaging. He stared at her, completely in awe.

She hadn't asked questions. She hadn't run away in fear. She had just... helped him.

And in that moment, he knew.

She was the one.

She was the one he wanted to spend the rest of his life with. The one he would move heaven and earth for. The one who had changed him in ways even magic never could.

But now, instead of being by his side, she was locked away in a dungeon because of him.

He clenched his jaw, his fists tightening.

He couldn't let this happen.

He had already failed her once. He wouldn't fail her again.

He had to do something to save her.

***

Layla sat in the cold, dark dungeon, her arms wrapped around herself for warmth. She had been trying to think of a way out, a way to clear her name, a way to convince the court that she wasn't the villain in this grand mess.

But no matter how hard she tried to focus, her mind kept drifting back to him.

The Prince of Isfahan.

His face flashed in her memory—the way his shoulders had dropped, the way his jaw had tensed, the way his eyes had darkened when the King ordered her imprisonment. That wasn't the face of a man who had won. That was the face of a man who had just lost something precious.

Did he not want her to get hurt?

Had he been telling the truth when he said he loved her?

Layla hated this uncertainty. She had always been good at spotting deception, at knowing when someone was playing a game. And yet, right now, she couldn't tell the truth apart from the lies. She wanted to believe she had been right to expose him. She wanted to believe he was just another privileged prince who thought he could toy with a woman's heart and walk away without consequences.

But then... why did she feel guilty?

The thought unsettled her.

She had spent so much energy tearing apart his reputation, making sure the entire court turned against him. But what if she had been wrong? What if he didn't deserve it?

Layla let out a long sigh, leaning her head back against the stone wall.

And, as much as she didn't want to admit it, she wasn't lying when she said the Prince had broken her heart.

Because the truth was, she had started falling for him.

She remembered the secret meetings—the thrill of sneaking away just to see him. His ridiculous jokes, the way his eyes lit up when he teased her, the way he made her blush with just a glance.

She had spent so much time convincing herself that he was a scoundrel, that he was only playing a game, that he was just another prince who thought he could have whatever he wanted. But deep down, she had enjoyed every moment with him.

And oh, how could she forget about the smiling moon? The moon never smiled at Layla until that night. The night she met the Prince of Isfahan for the first time. What if all of this was connected together?

Her thoughts were interrupted by a sudden noise.

The soft flutter of wings.

Layla's eyes snapped to the small, barred window of her dungeon cell. A white dove had landed on the narrow ledge, its tiny claws gripping the cold stone.

For a second, Layla thought she was imagining things.

But then, the dove opened its claws and let a small, folded piece of parchment drop onto the floor.

She scrambled to her feet and rushed forward to grab it.

The bird, as if its job was done, flapped its wings again and disappeared into the night.

Layla barely noticed. She was too busy unfolding the note, her fingers trembling slightly as she smoothed out the delicate parchment.

Four words were written on it.

"Truth is the cure."

Layla froze.

The handwriting.

It was the same as the one on the letter written in blood.

Her breath caught in her throat.

Could it be him?

Could it really be the Prince of Isfahan?

Her fingers traced the ink on the parchment, as if touching it would somehow make the answer clearer.

Doves represented fidelity. That was a fact known across kingdoms. They were symbols of love, loyalty, and devotion.

Was this a sign?

Did the Prince send her a message?

Her heart pounded in her chest.

He most definitely did.

Layla sat in the dim dungeon, reading the message over and over again.

"Truth is the cure."

What truth?

The Prince of Isfahan must have meant something specific, but what was it?

She tried to think.

The King of Isfahan had been against her from the start. He had never trusted her. He saw her as a threat the moment his son showed interest in her.

But why?

Why had he been so quick to condemn her? Was it really just about his son's reputation? Or was there something more?

Layla clenched her jaw. The King had accused her, judged her, and sentenced her without so much as giving her a chance to speak in her own defense.

If only she could force him to listen.

That's when an idea struck her.

A wild, risky, impossible idea.

But it just might work.

Layla knew that the King of Isfahan wasn't just an ordinary ruler. He was paranoid. He was suspicious of outsiders, of spies, of anything that might threaten his kingdom. And there was one thing that could make him stop and reconsider before ordering her execution.

A secret that would make her too important to kill.

She would claim to be a Mossad agent.

The thought sent a chill down her spine.

It was dangerous. Very dangerous.

But the more she thought about it, the more it made sense.

She wasn't lying. Not really. She wasn't claiming to be something she wasn't—she was using the King's own fears against him. He already believed she was part of some conspiracy. He already saw her as a danger to his kingdom.

If she played her cards right, she could make him believe that executing her would be a mistake.

She took a deep breath, steadying herself.

She wasn't going to beg for mercy. She wasn't going to plead for her life.

She was going to make the King of Isfahan see her as someone he couldn't afford to get rid of.

Now, all she had to do was wait for her chance.

The next time the guards came with food, Layla knew this was the moment she had to act.

She refused to appear weak. If she begged or pleaded, they would only see her as a desperate woman trying to save her own skin. No—she had to be bold. She had to make them believe she was something more.

When the guard extended his arm to slide the tray of food through the iron bars, Layla moved swiftly. Her fingers closed around the rough fabric of his sleeve.

The guard flinched, startled by her sudden grip. He looked down at her with suspicion, ready to shove her away. But Layla tightened her hold, pulling him just slightly closer.

Then, in a low, icy whisper, she said, *"Tell your King if he orders my execution, the Mossad will come for him."*

The guard's face instantly paled. His grip on the tray wavered, and for a second, Layla thought he might drop it altogether. His throat bobbed as he swallowed hard, his eyes darting toward the entrance of the dungeon as if expecting someone to burst in at any moment.

Layla released his sleeve, watching as he stumbled back, his breathing uneven. He didn't say a word. He didn't even try to scold her for touching him.

Instead, without another glance, he turned on his heel and *ran*.

Layla exhaled slowly, forcing herself to remain calm.

For a brief moment, a wave of satisfaction washed over her. She had shaken him. That was good. That meant the King would hear her message.

But then, as the silence of the dungeon settled around her, a new feeling crept in.

What had she just done?

This was dangerous. Very dangerous.

She had no idea how the King would react. Would he be furious? Would he grow suspicious? Or worse… would he see through her bluff?

She stared down at the untouched food on the tray, suddenly losing her appetite.

***

In Jerusalem, the Prince of Jerusalem sat in his grand court, listening to the latest news brought by his most trusted informants. He had always been well-connected, and nothing that happened in the great kingdoms of the world escaped his ears. But today's news caught his attention more than usual.

Layla.

The girl who had once lived in the Palace of Babylon. The girl the King of Babylon had told him about in passing—an innocent soul, troubled in ways that made the world misunderstand her. The King had not described her as *mentally ill*—no, he had used kinder words. He had said she was *a girl with a delicate mind, one who saw the world differently from others.*

And now, she was imprisoned in Isfahan.

The Prince leaned back in his chair, rubbing his chin thoughtfully as he listened to the details. Apparently, Layla had caused quite the uproar in the royal court. First, she had exposed the Prince of Isfahan, turning half the kingdom against him. Then, she had been condemned to death by the King of Isfahan. And now?

Now, she had claimed to be a Mossad agent.

At that, the Prince of Jerusalem let out a quiet, amused laugh.

Only *she* would come up with something like that. Only a girl with a pure heart—one who didn't fully grasp the consequences of her words—would make such a bold claim without realizing the storm it would bring.

She had no idea what she had just done.

By mentioning Mossad, she had unknowingly provoked the King of Isfahan in the worst way possible. That man was already furious with her, but now? Now, he would see her as a serious threat.

The Prince of Jerusalem sighed. Something about Layla's story struck him. There was something almost *tragic* about it. A girl without a home, tossed between kingdoms like a leaf caught in the wind. People spoke of her as if she were either a foolish troublemaker or a cunning manipulator, but the Prince of Jerusalem wasn't so sure.

Maybe she was neither.

Maybe she was just a girl trying to survive in a world where power ruled over everything else.

He was about to dismiss his informants when another piece of news stopped him.

The Prince of Isfahan.

Apparently, whispers had spread through the courts about the Prince of Isfahan and Layla. The two had been seen together, their interactions laced with something deeper than mere acquaintance. Some called it an infatuation, others a scandal waiting to happen.

But the Prince of Jerusalem had been in politics long enough to recognize the signs.

This wasn't a fleeting attraction.

It was love.

Real, raw, and dangerous.

The Prince of Isfahan, for all his reputation as a charismatic and carefree royal, was not the kind of man who would risk his standing for just any woman. And yet, he had done so for Layla—over and over again.

And Layla? She might not even realize it yet, but she had already set fire to his heart.

The Prince of Jerusalem exhaled slowly, feeling a pang of concern. Royal love was rarely left untainted. The world of power and alliances was full of vultures—whispering ministers, ambitious nobles, and even kings who saw love as nothing more than a weapon to be wielded.

If this was more than just a rumor—if the Prince of Isfahan truly loved Layla—then the court would soon turn against them both.

He didn't know whether their love would survive the storm, but he knew one thing for certain:

He would not let royal politics destroy them.

He made his decision.

He would go to Isfahan.

Not just to save Layla—but to save them both.

***

Layla had lost count of the days.

The cold, damp walls of the dungeon had become her entire world, and with each passing moment, she felt her hope slipping away. No one had come for her. Not the Prince of Isfahan. Not anyone from Babylon. And certainly not Mossad—though, in hindsight, she realized how foolish it had been to expect that her bluff would work.

The guards had stopped reacting to her entirely. They came, dropped her food, and left without a word. She had tried speaking to them once or twice, but they either ignored her or gave her cold, empty stares.

Perhaps this was it.

Perhaps she would die here, forgotten.

But then, one morning, something changed.

The guards entered her cell, but this time, they didn't come with food. Instead, they grabbed her by the arms and pulled her up.

"What's going on?" Layla asked, trying to sound strong, but her voice came out weaker than she intended.

The guards didn't answer. They simply dragged her forward, their grips firm, their expressions unreadable.

Layla's heart pounded as they led her up the stone steps, through the long corridors of the palace, and into the grand court.

And there, standing before her, were two men.

One was the King of Isfahan, sitting stiffly on his throne, his face carved from stone. He didn't even look at her.

The other was the Prince of Jerusalem. Unlike the King of Isfahan, he didn't ignore Layla. He turned his head slightly, meeting her eyes, and gave her the smallest of nods.

It was barely noticeable. Just the slightest movement. But in that moment, it spoke volumes.

Everything will be fine.

Layla exhaled, not realizing she had been holding her breath.

But then, her gaze flickered back to the King of Isfahan, and her stomach twisted. He still refused to look at her. He stared straight ahead, his fingers drumming against the armrest of his throne.

The silence in the room was suffocating.

Layla had no idea what was about to happen. But she knew one thing—this was her only chance.

The tension in the court was thick enough to cut with a blade.

The King of Isfahan finally shifted in his throne, his sharp gaze landing on the Prince of Jerusalem. His expression, usually unreadable, now showed clear disappointment.

"So, this is why you traveled all this way?" His voice was slow and measured, but the scorn was unmistakable. "Not to discuss the matters of kingdoms, not to strengthen alliances, but to plead for a prisoner?"

The Prince of Jerusalem didn't flinch. He met the King's gaze with steady calm, as if he had expected this reaction.

"I came because justice matters," he replied. "Even for a prisoner."

The King of Isfahan scoffed. "I thought you were a ruler of wisdom and sound judgment. That is why you hold the keys to Jerusalem," he said, his voice sharp with warning. "But now I wonder if I was wrong to believe that."

Layla felt a sinking guilt in her chest. She hadn't asked for this. She had spoken out of desperation, trying to buy herself time. Yet here stood the Prince of Jerusalem, risking the delicate balance of power—risking his own authority—for her.

But he remained unshaken. Instead of backing down, he took a step forward. "Your Majesty, you underestimate the danger of this situation."

The King narrowed his eyes. "Danger?"

The Prince of Jerusalem nodded. "You see only a foolish girl who has stirred trouble. But have you considered what might happen if you execute her?" His voice lowered slightly, just enough to stir unease. "What if her claims are true?"

A murmur spread through the court.

The King's expression hardened. "Ridiculous. She is a girl from Babylon, nothing more."

The Prince of Jerusalem let out a quiet breath, almost amused. "Are you certain?" His tone was careful, but the challenge was clear. "She appeared in Babylon with no past, no family. And yet, she found herself under the protection of the King of Babylon. Doesn't that strike you as... strange?"

The murmurs grew louder.

Layla stiffened. What was the Prince doing? He was treading a dangerous line, shifting the weight of the conversation into something else entirely.

The King of Isfahan shifted in his seat.

"You are playing a dangerous game," he warned.

"I am stating facts," the Prince of Jerusalem replied smoothly. "If Layla truly has ties to the Mossad, her execution will not be ignored. You may not fear her—but do you fear what follows her?"

Silence fell over the room.

Layla held her breath.

She had never meant to deceive anyone. She wasn't a liar. But the way the Prince of Jerusalem spoke, the way he made her sound like a mystery that even kings should be wary of... it made her seem like something more than just a girl caught in the wrong place at the wrong time.

And the King of Isfahan was listening.

He wasn't convinced—not yet. But he wasn't dismissing it either.

The court fell into hushed whispers as the heavy doors creaked open once more.

The Prince of Isfahan stepped into the grand hall. His usual charm and wit were nowhere to be seen. His eyes, dark with something unspoken, flickered between Layla and his father.

Layla, still kneeling before the throne, held her breath.

The tension in the room was thick. The King of Isfahan straightened, sensing the shift. The Prince of Jerusalem—who had just risked everything to defend Layla—stood silently, watching closely.

Then, the Prince of Isfahan spoke.

"This trial is unnecessary," he declared. "Because Layla is using the Saladin strategy."

A wave of whispers spread through the court. Even the King of Isfahan, usually composed, looked momentarily taken aback.

Layla blinked in confusion. *Saladin?*

Everyone knew the name. Saladin Ayyubi—the warrior who reclaimed Jerusalem from the Crusaders. A master of both battle and diplomacy. He had not only defeated kings but had *won them over*. Instead of ruling through fear, he had united rival factions, bringing them under his command with promises of peace.

The King of Isfahan's shock quickly turned to anger. His hands clenched the armrests of his throne. "Enough of this nonsense," he snapped. "What trickery are you speaking of now?"

The Prince of Isfahan did not back down.

"This is no trick, Father," he said. "This is the truth you refuse to see." His gaze swept the room. "Has anyone questioned why Layla was under the King of Babylon's protection? Why she carries herself with such confidence, even now, facing death? Why the Prince of Jerusalem, who holds the keys to the Holy City, would risk his position to defend her?"

The King of Isfahan let out a sharp breath, eyes narrowing. "You mean to tell me... she seeks to do what Saladin did?" His voice grew sharper. "To unite powerful men under her banner? To turn kings into her allies, and to take what is not hers?" He pointed an accusing finger at Layla. "You think you can play us all like pieces on a board?"

Layla's heart pounded.

Next, the Prince of Jerusalem stepped forward. "That is an unfair accusation, Your Majesty," he said smoothly. "Layla is no conqueror, but she is wise enough to forge alliances. And you forget one thing—Saladin did not take Jerusalem by force alone. He was offered the city by those who saw his wisdom." He let the words settle. "And perhaps, just *perhaps*, the same wisdom should be considered here."

Everyone present in the court gasped. The implication was clear.

The Prince of Jerusalem was not just defending Layla. He was suggesting that *she*—a girl from Babylon—might one day hold *the keys to Jerusalem*.

The King of Isfahan's fury was instant. His voice was sharp as a blade. "You would offer Jerusalem to *her*?"

The Prince of Jerusalem met his gaze evenly. "I said no such thing." He smiled, though there was steel beneath it. "I only suggest that Jerusalem has always been ruled by those who understand its importance. And if Layla has gained such favor, then perhaps she deserves a place among those who decide its fate."

The room was in chaos now.

Layla held her breath, keeping her face still.

The Prince of Isfahan smirked and said, "So... she's *Saladin* now?"

The Prince of Jerusalem didn't miss a beat. He simply smiled and lifted a hand.

"Seize him."

The room froze.

The King of Isfahan shot to his feet.

Guards hesitated, looking between each other, unsure if they'd heard correctly. The Prince of Isfahan blinked, then raised his hands in mock surrender. "Well, that's a bold move."

The Prince of Jerusalem remained serious. "You think this is a game, but you know exactly what she's done. She played her cards right, and she won." He tilted his head. "You saw it before anyone else. That's why you're making jokes instead of denying it."

The King of Isfahan's eyes darkened. His son was in danger—because of a *woman*?

Layla stayed quiet. The room felt like it was shifting beneath her feet, and she knew better than to interrupt.

The Prince of Isfahan let out a short laugh. "You know," he said, looking at Layla, "I'd almost be jealous—if I wasn't so impressed."

Then he turned back to his father. "You see what's happening, don't you?" His voice was lighter, but his eyes were sharp. "She played her hand so well that *they're* willing to turn on *me* for her." He let out a breath. "That's not the kind of woman you kill, Father. That's the kind of woman you *fear*."

A long silence followed.

Then, finally, the King of Isfahan exhaled.

"Release him," he said.

The guards stepped back.

The King of Isfahan exhaled sharply, gripping the arms of his throne. "And what proof do you have that she is worthy of such power?"

The Prince of Jerusalem looked at the Prince of Isfahan. Maybe he should let him answer this one.

The Prince of Isfahan hesitated but did not falter. "I have no proof," he admitted. "Only certainty."

The King scoffed. "Then your certainty is worthless."

The Prince of Jerusalem chuckled. It was not loud, nor mocking, but it was enough.

He stepped forward, tilting his head slightly. "Fascinating," he mused. "Because if Layla is playing the Saladin strategy, then what does that make you, Prince of Isfahan?" His gaze flickered, his lips curling into something dangerously close to a smirk. "Are you her greatest ally? Or just another piece on her board?"

The Prince of Isfahan's jaw tightened.

Layla saw it then—the game shifting, the tables turning. The Prince of Jerusalem was not defending her out of kindness alone.

He was playing his own move.

Layla had flirted with power before. She had walked the line between strength and destruction. But this—this—was something different.

The Prince of Jerusalem was forcing the Prince of Isfahan into a corner. Daring him to reveal his hand.

And the Prince of Isfahan—a man who had never before been trapped—fell right into it.

He exhaled sharply. His fingers curled into fists. Then, finally, his voice rang through the hall.

"I love her."

A stunned silence filled the room.

Layla's breath caught in her throat.

The King's gaze sharpened. His anger flickered into something more dangerous—calculation.

The Prince of Isfahan continued. "If she were a deceiver, she would have played me for a fool long ago. But she hasn't. If she were unworthy, I would have forgotten her. But I haven't." He took a steady breath. "Father, I love her."

A long, heavy silence followed.

The King of Isfahan studied his son, as if searching for a lie. Then, slowly, he leaned back into his throne.

His fingers tapped against the armrest. His mind was working, calculating the consequences.

Layla met his gaze. She did not shrink away. Despite the storm of emotions inside her, she forced herself to remain steady.

The King turned back to his son. "You would risk everything for this girl?"

The Prince of Isfahan did not hesitate. "Yes."

The King exhaled. His expression softened—just a fraction. Then, finally, he nodded.

"Then so be it." He waved a hand at the guards. "Take her from the dungeon. Give her a chamber fitting of her new position."

The guards hesitated, unsure if they had heard correctly.

The King's voice grew firm. "She is not to be harmed." He paused, then added, "If the Mossad has claimed her, then we must reconsider how we see her."

Layla barely had time to process what had happened before the guards were already moving.

She was being led away—not back to the darkness of the dungeon, but to something entirely different.

As she walked, she stole a glance at the Prince of Isfahan.

His eyes met hers.

And in that moment, she knew—this was not the end. This was only the beginning.

Chapter 11: The Crown

Once alone in her chamber, Layla began pacing. She couldn't think straight. What had just happened? Did they really just convince the King of Isfahan to accept her for his son? Or was she just a pawn in a much bigger game? Had she won her freedom—or was she in more danger than ever?

She ran a hand through her hair, frustration building in her chest. Everything had moved too fast. Then—*knock, knock.*

She jumped, her pulse spiking. For a brief second, panic gripped her. Then she straightened. Whoever it was, she wouldn't let them see her shaken.

She opened the door. Standing there, wearing that same infuriating smirk, was the Prince of Isfahan.

"Miss me already?" he asked, leaning casually against the doorframe.

Layla folded her arms. "If I say no, will you leave?"

He grinned. "No." Then, before she could respond, he stepped inside, shutting the door behind him.

Layla raised an eyebrow. "Bold move."

"Seems to be the theme of the day," he said, glancing around her chamber. "Nice. Cozy. Not exactly a dungeon, is it?"

She sighed. "What do you want?"

His expression softened just slightly. "To talk."

She hesitated but didn't stop him when he walked further into the room. She stayed near the door, arms still crossed, waiting.

For the first time since she had met him, he looked... uncertain. Not entirely, of course—he was still the same arrogant prince who flirted even in the face of war. But there was something else in his eyes now.

Something *real*.

"I suppose," he started, "I should begin with an apology."

Layla raised an eyebrow. "You? Apologizing?"

"Shocking, I know," he said with a small smile. Then he exhaled. "But I mean it. For the misunderstandings, for the games, for..." He gestured vaguely. "Everything."

Layla studied him. "What changed?"

He hesitated. Then, after a moment, he shrugged. "Maybe I realized that you're not just playing the game. You *are* the game." He smirked. "And I lost."

Layla let out a small, breathy laugh. "That's a first."

His smile lingered, but his gaze turned serious.

"My father won't harm you now," he said. "Not with the Prince of Jerusalem on your side. He might not like you, but he *does* like keeping his political alliances intact. If hurting you means losing an ally in Jerusalem, he won't risk it."

Layla processed that for a moment.

"So I'm safe," she murmured.

"For now," he admitted.

She exhaled. It wasn't perfect, but it was better than she had hoped for just hours ago.

She looked up at him again, something softer in her gaze now. "And you?" she asked. "Where do you stand in all of this?"

The Prince of Isfahan tilted his head slightly, watching her.

Then, he took a step closer.

"I think," he said, voice quieter now, "that I stopped trying to figure that out the moment I met you."

Layla's breath caught, but she forced herself to stay composed.

"Was that supposed to be a confession?" she asked, tilting her chin up slightly.

He smirked. "If it was, would you believe me?"

She hesitated. Then, finally, she smiled.

"I think," she said, "that I don't need to hear it to *know* it."

Something flickered in his eyes—something deep, something unspoken.

For a moment, neither of them moved.

Then, just as quickly as the moment had come, he stepped back, his usual playful smirk returning.

"Well," he said, "don't go falling for me too quickly. I quite like the chase."

Layla rolled her eyes. "You'd be insufferable if it were too easy."

He laughed. Then, with a lingering glance, he turned toward the door.

"Get some rest, Layla," he said. "This isn't over yet."

And with that, he was gone. Layla let out a slow breath, placing a hand over her chest. No, this wasn't over.

Days passed.

Layla had no idea what was happening beyond the walls of her chamber.

She tried asking the guards, but they remained silent. The female servant assigned to her came and went, bringing her food, fresh clothes, and little else. No news. No messages.

The waiting was unbearable.

Had the King of Isfahan decided to let her go? Or was he planning something worse?

She hated feeling powerless. But there was nothing she could do except wait.

One morning, just as she was finishing her breakfast, her servant entered the room carrying fine silks and golden jewelry.

Layla frowned.

"What is this?" she asked.

The servant set the items down on the bed and bowed her head. "His Majesty expects to see you," she said. "You must be dressed properly."

Layla's stomach tightened.

This was it.

She had spent days wondering what the King would do. Now, she was finally going to find out.

The servant helped her into a deep blue dress embroidered with golden patterns. It was finer than anything she had worn since arriving in Isfahan. The jewelry was light but elegant—golden bracelets, earrings, and a delicate chain around her forehead.

When Layla looked at herself in the mirror, she barely recognized the woman staring back.

Her servant, seeing her hesitation, gave a small smile.

"You look like a queen," she said softly.

Layla swallowed hard. A queen? She wasn't sure if she was walking toward a throne or a prison.

***

The royal hall was vast and intimidating.

Columns lined the sides, each carved with stories of battles and victories. Golden chandeliers hung high above, their candlelight flickering like stars. At the far end sat the King of Isfahan, dressed in deep red robes, a golden crown resting on his head.

Layla kept her steps steady as she approached. She would not let him see her fear.

She stopped before him and bowed slightly, just enough to be respectful.

The King studied her for a long moment, then leaned back in his chair.

"Do you know," he said, "that if you were anyone else, you would have been executed by now?"

His words were calm, but there was arrogance beneath them.

Layla did not respond. She simply held his gaze.

The King exhaled sharply. "Your alliances have forced me to reconsider my position." He shook his head. "It is not often that a mere girl manages to make powerful men hesitate. The Prince of Jerusalem, the King of Babylon, and even my own son—each of them has risked much for you."

Layla remained silent. She would not play into his games.

The King's eyes narrowed. "Tell me, Layla—what have you done to them?"

She lifted her chin. "Nothing but be myself."

The King scoffed. "Then that is a dangerous thing to be."

His voice was sharp now. "Do you know what kind of chaos you could cause? A woman who turns kings into allies? A woman who makes enemies question their choices? That is power, Layla. And power is dangerous when it is not controlled."

Layla clenched her fists at her sides, but before she could speak, another voice cut through the tension.

"Father, please."

The room fell into silence.

Layla turned—so did the King.

The Prince of Isfahan had stepped forward.

For the first time, the arrogant, playful glint in his eyes was gone. He looked serious. Determined.

The King frowned. "What did you say?"

The Prince took another step closer. "I said please," he repeated, his voice firm. "Enough of this. Let this end."

Layla's breath caught.

The King stared at his son as if he were seeing him for the first time.

"You dare interrupt me?" he asked.

The Prince did not waver. "Yes."

A heavy silence filled the hall.

Then, slowly, the King leaned forward, his eyes sharp with curiosity. "Tell me, son—how far are you willing to go for this girl?"

The Prince did not hesitate. "As far as it takes."

The King studied him, then nodded slowly. "Very well."

He leaned back in his chair. "If you are so certain, then prove it."

***

The King began his test. He asked the Prince a series of questions—some about Layla, some about himself.

"Do you understand the risk you are taking?"

"Yes."

"Would you defy your father for her?"

"If I must."

"Would you still stand by her if she lost every alliance?"

"I would stand by her even if the world stood against us."

The King's gaze darkened. "And if I told you that choosing her would cost you the throne?"

The Prince hesitated—just for a second. Then he lifted his chin.

"Then I will build a kingdom of my own."

Layla felt her chest tighten. The King's expression remained unreadable, but there was something like amusement in his eyes. He turned to Layla.

"And you?" he asked. "Would you stand beside my son?"

Layla met his gaze. "I would."

His expression remained still. "Even if it meant becoming a queen in a land that was never yours?"

Layla didn't look away. "I have never been afraid of stepping into the unknown."

The King's fingers drummed against the armrest of his throne. Then, finally, he exhaled. "Very well," he said. "Then you shall be wed."

Layla's heart pounded.

"On the night of the full moon," the King declared, "you will become husband and wife."

The court murmured in shock. Layla turned to the Prince of Isfahan.

He was already looking at her.

He smiled—this time, not his usual playful smirk, but something real. Something meant only for her.

***

The city of Isfahan had never seen such a grand occasion.

As the news of the royal wedding spread, the people rejoiced. The streets, which once whispered uncertainties about Layla, now murmured with admiration. Some spoke of her beauty, others of the Prince's devotion, but most spoke of her wisdom—how a young woman, in the face of kings, had turned the tides in her favor.

The King of Isfahan, though proud and severe, had allowed the marriage to proceed, and in doing so, he had granted his son a rare gift—the right to choose.

But for Layla, this was no ordinary wedding. It was a symbol of diplomacy, of alliances forged not with swords but with intellect. She knew that all eyes were on her—not just the nobility of Isfahan but also the Prince of Jerusalem, whose silent gaze had followed her carefully ever since.

In the days leading to the ceremony, the entire city transformed into a garden of lilies.

From the grand palace courtyards to the smallest alleyways, white lilies bloomed in full splendor, their soft petals swaying in the cool desert breeze. It was said that lilies were Layla's favorite, though no one knew how the people had learned this.

Some believed it was the work of the Prince of Isfahan, who had insisted on honoring his bride. Others thought it was the people themselves, charmed by the woman who had captured their prince's heart.

Layla, from the high balcony of her chamber, looked upon the sea of white. A fragrance so pure and gentle filled the air that, for a moment, she forgot all her worries.

Yet, amid the celebration, Layla remained careful. She knew that marriage into the Isfahani court did not guarantee her safety. She had won the King's approval, but approval could be withdrawn as easily as it was given. And so, she continued to play her role with grace and wisdom.

One evening, as she sat in the palace gardens, surrounded by noblewomen, she was asked to speak.

"Tell us, Layla," one of the women asked, "what does it mean to be a queen?"

Layla smiled as she traced the rim of her cup, thinking for a moment. The women around her leaned in, waiting for her answer.

"A queen," she said, "shines like the rays of the sun—warm, bright, and full of life. She does not keep her light to herself but spreads it to those around her, just like the sun gives warmth to the earth. A true queen lifts her people, giving them hope, strength, and guidance."

She paused, then continued.

"But a queen can also be like the moon. When the night is dark and the world feels uncertain, she must shine even brighter. The moon does not have its own light, but it still lights up the night sky. In the same way, a queen must bring hope to her people, even in the hardest times."

One of the women hesitated before asking, "But what if the sun burns too hot? What if the night is too long?"

Layla's expression softened. "Then a queen must know when to be strong and when to be gentle. Sometimes, she must be like the midday sun, powerful and unshakable. Other times, she must be like the moon, calm and steady, giving comfort when it is needed. A wise queen knows how to balance both."

The women nodded, her words settling in their hearts. In that moment, they no longer saw Layla as just a woman in their company.

They saw her as a queen.

The women listened, nodding thoughtfully.

But one man, standing beneath the shade of a nearby tree, listened even more intently.

The Prince of Jerusalem.

Though he said nothing, his dark eyes remained fixed on Layla. He had known many women—some more beautiful, some more powerful—but none quite like her.

She was neither timid nor aggressive, neither silent nor arrogant. She knew when to speak and when to hold her tongue. And that was true power.

The Prince of Jerusalem watched as she moved from conversation to conversation, winning hearts not with flattery, but with wisdom. He knew then that Layla was more than just the future queen of Isfahan. She was a force of nature—one that the world had yet to fully understand.

***

At last, the wedding night arrived.

The palace shone under the silver glow of the full moon. Every corner was lit with golden lanterns, their flames flickering like stars. Musicians played soft melodies in the background, and the scent of lilies filled the air.

The Prince of Isfahan stood tall at the entrance of the great hall, dressed in fine silks embroidered with gold. His usual smirk was absent tonight—replaced by something deeper, something real.

And then, she arrived.

Layla, adorned in a flowing gown of ivory and gold, her veil as delicate as morning mist, entered the hall. Her eyes, lined with kohl, held a quiet strength as she walked with measured grace.

The Nikkah ceremony was conducted in the presence of esteemed guests. Scholars, nobles, and kings alike bore witness as the Qadi (Islamic judge) began the sacred recitations.

Layla and the Prince of Isfahan were seated separately at first, as tradition dictated. A white silk sheet was placed between them—a symbol of modesty and purity.

The Qadi turned to the Prince first.

"Do you, son of the King of Isfahan, accept Layla as your wife, in accordance with the laws of Allah and His Messenger?"

The room fell silent.

The Prince of Isfahan raised his head, his voice steady. "I do."

The Qadi then turned to Layla, who sat with her hands folded gently in her lap.

"Do you, Layla, daughter of the East, accept this man as your husband, in accordance with the laws of Allah and His Messenger?"

For a moment, Layla said nothing.

Not because she was uncertain, but because she understood the weight of this moment.

Then, with quiet certainty, she spoke.

"I do."

A wave of murmurs spread through the hall—some in admiration, some in shock.

It was rare for a woman to speak with such confidence in such a setting.

The Prince of Jerusalem, seated among the guests, smiled slightly.

She had done it again.

She had taken a simple moment and turned it into something unforgettable.

After the wedding feast, when the last of the songs had been sung and the final blessings had been recited, the Prince of Jerusalem rose from his seat.

All eyes turned to him.

Slowly, he stepped forward until he stood before Layla.

His expression was unreadable, his gaze steady. Then, in a voice that echoed through the hall, he said:

"Let it be known that from this night forward, Layla shall have the keys to Jerusalem."

Gasps filled the air. Even the King of Isfahan raised an eyebrow.

The keys to Jerusalem?

That was no ordinary gift. That was a symbol of trust, of power, of something far greater than gold or land.

Layla herself was taken aback.

She looked up at the Prince of Jerusalem, searching his face for an explanation.

He gave her a small, knowing smile.

"May your wisdom guide not just this kingdom, but all who seek it," he said.

Layla bowed her head in gratitude.

She understood what he was saying without words.

This was not just a gift.

It was a challenge.

A kingdom had just been placed in her hands. Now, the question was—what would she do with it?

***

Far away from the grand city of Isfahan, deep in the silent desert, a lonely figure sat under a rocky ledge, staring into the distance.

The Behemoth of Alcoholia had just heard the news.

Layla—the girl he had spent years teasing, tricking, and mocking—was now a princess.

She had married the Prince of Isfahan.

The Behemoth of Alcoholia clenched his jaw, his fingers digging into the sand.

He had always laughed at her, making her stumble over rocks, whispering in her ear to startle her, leading her in circles when she wandered the desert. He had told himself she was nothing special—just an ordinary girl, just Layla.

And yet, somehow, she had proven him wrong.

The whole world was talking about her. The brave, clever Layla, who had outsmarted kings, won the heart of a prince, and secured her place in history.

Meanwhile, he was nothing now. Just a fugitive. Just a shadow, hiding for his life.

Fate was strange indeed.

Chapter 12: The Endgame

The Prince of Jerusalem was a legend. He had the kind of wisdom people wrote stories about, the kind of bravery that made soldiers follow him into battles no one thought they could win. His integrity was unquestionable, his justice fair, and his courage unshakable. People trusted him with their lives, their families, and their city. If the Prince of Jerusalem made a decision, everyone believed it was the right one. It was as simple as that.

But when he handed over the keys to Jerusalem to Layla, the world paused for a moment. It wasn't the kind of decision anyone had expected. The Prince, the great and wise ruler of Jerusalem, now placed the most sacred symbol of the city into the hands of a woman, and not just any woman—a woman from Babylon, a place most people could barely locate on a map, let alone understand its ways.

At first, no one knew what to think. The court was silent, as if the very air had thickened with confusion. People in the streets whispered behind their hands. Some said, "He's lost his mind." Others were more certain: "The Prince must be sick. He needs to step down before things get worse."

Rumors spread like wildfire. "He's gone mad," they said, shaking their heads. "Everyone knew he was too young to rule. Who hands over the keys to a city to someone like her?"

But Layla? Layla didn't even bat an eye. She had lived her life being underestimated, being doubted. People didn't realize she had learned long ago how to make her silence speak louder than any words could.

She walked through the streets of Jerusalem, her head held high, but her steps quiet. She didn't need to make speeches. She didn't need to prove anyone wrong by arguing. Instead, she set to work, quietly, efficiently. She spoke to the people, not as a ruler, but as someone who truly listened. When a small merchant asked for her attention, she gave it. When a beggar reached out for help, she found a way to make sure they weren't ignored. She did the little things that no one ever notices unless they were done wrong.

The people started to notice. The merchants saw that their trade routes flourished under her watch. The scholars realized she was opening the gates for knowledge, bringing in new ideas from across the lands. Even the soldiers found themselves standing taller, proud to defend a city they now felt had a future.

As the years passed, the whispers from the marketplace grew softer. "She knows what she's doing," they said, nodding as they watched her speak calmly with the high priests. "Maybe this was the right choice after all."

But the true test came when an outsider tried to take advantage of the city's brief moment of weakness. A cunning man with a fast tongue and an even faster hand, who thought he could seize the opportunity to make a name for himself. He tried to rattle the city's foundations with threats and deceit, but Layla was ready. She didn't rush into battle, didn't even call her soldiers. No, she did something far simpler and far more effective.

She sat across from him, calm and composed. And with a few carefully chosen words, a smile that didn't reach her eyes, and a promise to make him regret ever thinking of taking Jerusalem, she left him with no choice but to slink back into the shadows from where he came. No one raised a sword. There was no need. Layla had outsmarted him, with nothing more than her wit.

And just like that, Layla proved them all wrong.

She didn't just hold the keys to Jerusalem; she had the heart of the city.

The whispers grew into applause. People began to understand that the Prince of Jerusalem had done the right thing after all. They saw the power of patience, wisdom, and quiet strength. "She's not like the others," they said. "She's got a different kind of power, one that doesn't need to shout or fight to be heard."

Meanwhile, in the Kingdom of Arabia, the Prince of Arabia was on a mission. His heart burned with anger and determination, for the Behemoth of Alcoholic had wronged Layla. The demon had hurt her in ways that only he could understand, and the Prince of Arabia was set on finding him. He was determined to bring the Behemoth to justice, to make him pay for what he did to Layla.

But what started as a quest for justice slowly twisted into something different. The Prince of Arabia wasn't trying to hurt Layla—his intentions were pure. But the people, well, they didn't see it that way. The rumors began to spread, like wildfire, growing bigger and louder with each passing day.

It started small. Just a whisper here and there. Maybe they had seen Layla and the Prince of Arabia speaking in the halls, exchanging words that could be misinterpreted. Maybe someone overheard a quiet laugh or saw a gesture that seemed a little too intimate. The next thing they knew, the whispers were everywhere.

People started saying things like, "Did you hear about Layla and the Prince of Arabia? They must have something going on." And with that, the rumors grew. Some said that Layla and the Prince of Arabia were having an affair behind the back of the Prince of Isfahan. Others said the Prince of Arabia had been trying to steal her away, playing a game of power and seduction.

Layla, of course, had no part in these rumors. Her love for the Prince of Isfahan was real, pure, and unbreakable. She had never once looked at the Prince of Arabia with anything more than respect for his strength and determination. She understood his need to protect, and she appreciated him for it. But the truth was, her heart belonged to the Prince of Isfahan, and nothing—not the rumors, not the lies—could ever change that.

But still, the people didn't stop talking. They painted her as a traitor, accusing her of betraying the Prince of Isfahan. The whispers grew louder, harsher. The truth didn't matter to them anymore—only the story they wanted to believe.

Layla tried to ignore the gossip, but it wasn't easy. Everywhere she went, people would look at her with eyes full of judgment. Even the most casual glance from someone she'd once trusted now felt like an accusation. But she refused to let it break her. She had to stand tall. She knew the truth, and the Prince of Isfahan knew it too. That was all that mattered.

The Prince of Isfahan, of course, knew his heart. He trusted Layla with everything. He knew the rumors were just that—rumors. He didn't believe for a second that Layla had betrayed him. He had seen the way she looked at him, the way she fought beside him, and how deeply they cared for each other. Their love wasn't something that could be shattered by lies or rumors. It was built on trust and shared values.

But even with the Prince of Isfahan's trust, the rumors continued. People couldn't seem to stop themselves from talking, and soon the whispers began to turn into accusations. They said the Prince of Arabia was only after Layla because of jealousy, that his desire for revenge on the Behemoth of Alcoholic was just an excuse to get close to her. It didn't matter that he had never shown any romantic interest in Layla; the rumors had a life of their own now, and they spread like wildfire.

And still, the three of them—Layla, the Prince of Isfahan, and the Prince of Arabia—were all innocent. None of them were guilty of what the people were saying. Layla loved the Prince of Isfahan, and the Prince of Arabia had nothing but respect for her. The Prince of Isfahan trusted them both, and they all stood united in the face of the lies surrounding them.

The Kingdom of Isfahan, however, wasn't the only place where the story was being told. In Jerusalem, the people began to see Layla not just as the beloved of the Prince of Isfahan but also as a symbol of justice. She had stood up for what was right, she had defended the truth, and now, despite all the rumors, she continued to rule with fairness and wisdom.

The Lily fields that Layla and the Prince of Isfahan had planted together in the name of their love began to bloom, year after year, a quiet but strong reminder of their bond. Their love wasn't perfect, but it was real. It was unshakeable. And through all the trials, they both knew that they were in it together.

In the end, the rumors were forgotten, just as rumors always are. People began to see the truth—the Prince of Arabia's quest was never about love, but about justice. Layla's love for the Prince of Isfahan was never in doubt. And the three of them moved forward, united in the knowledge that their love, their actions, and their hearts would always remain true.

Years passed, and Layla continued to rule over Jerusalem with wisdom, kindness, and strength. She was not just a queen; she was a symbol of hope, justice, and love. Her marriage to the Prince of Isfahan remained strong, a partnership built on trust, respect, and deep affection. Together, they had weathered many storms, and together they had nurtured a kingdom where peace and prosperity flourished.

But no matter how strong one is, time catches up. Layla fell ill. At first, it was just a little fatigue, the kind that could be ignored. But soon, it became clear that this was no ordinary illness. She grew weaker by the day, her once vibrant face now pale and drawn. Her body seemed to waste away, as if life itself was slipping from her fingers. The doctors were puzzled; no medicine could heal her.

It was a sickness beyond their understanding, and soon, the people of Jerusalem began to fear the worst.

Layla, never one to complain, remained strong. But deep inside, she began to pray for peace. For solace. For an end to her suffering. She had given everything for the kingdom, for her love, for her people. And now, it seemed her time had come.

One quiet evening, as Layla lay in bed, unable to find rest, something extraordinary happened. In her final moments, unable to eat or drink, her eyes fluttered open one last time. In front of her, she saw a portrait of the Queen of England. And to her amazement, the Queen's image seemed to come to life. The Queen stepped out of the frame, her gentle smile as comforting as before.

"You are free now, Layla," the Queen whispered. "It's time to rest, and let your love live forever."

Layla felt herself being lifted, her spirit floating upward. She felt light, unburdened, and as if she were walking on air. She knew she was leaving behind the world, but she was not alone. As her spirit left her body, she recited the Shahadah softly, her voice a whisper in the air: "There is no god but Allah, and Muhammad is His messenger."

And as she was taken into the light, she knew her journey wasn't over—it was just beginning.

But as Layla's spirit departed, whispers began to spread throughout the kingdom. They said that her illness had been caused by her unfaithfulness to the Prince of Isfahan. Some accused her of being in love with another, that she had betrayed the Prince. People talked, and the gossip grew louder. The rumors said that her sickness was punishment for her sins, for a betrayal no one had ever seen but everyone had imagined.

Layla had been so much more than that, but the world didn't understand. The world never understood the love she shared with her Prince, nor did they know the strength she had inside her. They saw only the surface, and that was all they wanted to see.

Meanwhile, the Prince of Isfahan was far from home, on a business trip. He had no idea that his beloved Layla was slipping away. He was busy with matters of the kingdom, unaware of the sorrow that was unfolding back in Jerusalem. But the moment he heard the news, he rushed back, his heart pounding with fear and dread.

He arrived to find the kingdom in mourning, but Layla was already gone. Her body was still, her once lively eyes closed forever. The Prince fell to his knees beside her, his heart breaking as he realized the love of his life was no more. The vessel of Layla, the queen who had ruled with grace and wisdom, was now empty. Her era had passed.

But Layla's legacy lived on. The mark of her love and justice would never fade. The people who had once whispered about her now realized the truth. Layla had been a symbol of hope, and her love for the Prince of Isfahan was the kind that could never be broken by rumors or slander. It was pure, unshakable, and eternal.

As the Prince mourned his loss, a beautiful surprise arrived from a distant admirer. A bundle of red roses was delivered to Layla's resting place, a final tribute from the Adorer, a high-profile fan who had adored Layla from afar. He had heard of her passing and, heartbroken, sent the roses to honor her memory. The message that came with the roses was simple but full of love: *"For Layla, whose love and grace will never be forgotten."*

The Prince looked at the roses, a symbol of the love and admiration Layla had earned from far and wide. He knew that even though she was gone, her spirit would live on forever. The lilies that Layla and he had once planted would continue to bloom each year, a reminder of their love, and the mark she had left on the world.

And as the years passed, Layla's story would remain—her legacy of love, justice, and loyalty would never fade. It would live forever, written in the hearts of all who knew her, a love that could never be touched by the rumors or the misunderstandings of the world.

www.ingramcontent.com/pod-product-compliance
Lightning Source LLC
Chambersburg PA
CBHW071203070526
44584CB00019B/2895